HORRIBLE HISTORIES

ANNUAL 2012

This book belongs to:

SCHOLASTIC

D1443690

Contents

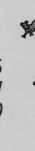

SAVAGE SHOWS & GORY SPORTS
History's most petrifying exercises.

Empire Games	5
Circus of Scares	6-7
Play and Slay	8-9
Undressed for Success	10-11
Bloody Ball Games	12-13
Highland Horrors	14

WOEFUL FOR WITCHES
Why some savage Stuarts were wicked to women.

Dreadful James	15
Trial and Terror	16-17
Which Witch?	18

SORRY FOR SOLDIERS
The nasty Napoleonic Wars.

Beastly Boney	19
Awful for Armies	20-21
Snow Way Home	22-23
Play 'Napoleon's Luck'!	24

AWFUL EXPLORERS
They went, they saw... they starved.

Terrible Travellers	25-27
Arctic Terror	28-29
Dress to Empress	30
Way Out West!	31
Up the Creek	32-33

LOUSY LIFESTYLES
Why it was putrid for the Victorian poor.

Bad for Beggars	34-35
Rotten Riverside	36-37
Cruel Schools	38-39
Street Strife	40

REVOLTING REVOLUTIONS
You won't be seeing Tsars round here!

Russian Riot	41-43
Bolshy Bother	44-45
Pitiful for Peasants	46-47
Red Riddles	48

AWFUL ENTERTAINMENT
Bad movies and some terrible moves!

Films, Flappers and Flights	49
Rockin' Riot	50-51
Silly Telly	52-53
Musical Bumps	54

SILLY CHILLY COLD WAR
It's East vs West – a terrifying test.

Frosty Face-Off	55-57
The Space Race	58-59

Answers 60-61

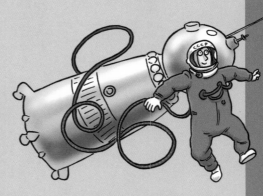

4

Empire Games

The Roman Emperors were potty about turning gory and gruesome games into massive spectator sports. Let's look at the awful early ADs to see why they did it...

THE RICH HIRED SLAVES TO DO THEIR WORK, SO ORDINARY ROMANS WERE PUT OUT OF WORK. TO STOP THEM CAUSING TROUBLE, EMPERORS GAVE THEM FREE FOOD AND GORY GAMES – "BREAD AND CIRCUSES".

PERSONALLY I PREFER BREAD AND CHEESE

ROME KEPT ADDING LANDS TO ITS EMPIRE. AFTER EMPEROR TRAJAN TRASHED DACIA (ROUND THE RIVER DANUBE), THE EMPIRE WAS AT ITS MOST ENORMOUS.

TRAJAN'S RAGIN!

A BIGGER EMPIRE MEANT BIGGER BORDERS WHICH MEANT MORE SOLDIERS. TO PAY FOR THEM, EMPEROR CARACALLA MADE EVERYONE IN THE EMPIRE A CITIZEN...

YOU'RE ALL CITIZENS NOW...

HOORAY!

SO HERE'S THE BILL

BOO!

...WHICH WAS A CLEVER WAY OF GETTING THEM TO PAY MORE TAX!

TO KEEP THE CITIZENS HAPPY, THE EMPERORS LAID ON MORE EXOTIC AND GRISLY GAMES. BUT MORE GORE SOON BECAME A BORE!

THESE MODERN SHOWS ARE ALL SPECIAL EFFECTS!

WAT–ER SPECTACLE!

THE GAMES CHANGED WHEN CONSTANTINE WAS EMPEROR. HE MADE CHRISTIANITY THE TOP RELIGION, SO CHRISTIANS WEREN'T THROWN TO THE LIONS ANY MORE.

?!?!

YOU CAN'T KILL ME, I'M A CHRISTIAN

THAT WASN'T THE ONLY GAME THAT CHANGED UNER CONSTANTINE. HE MOVED THE IMPERIAL CAPITAL TO THE EAST END OF THE EMPIRE, AND HAD A NEW CITY BUILT – A SORT OF ROME FROM HOME.

CREEP!

I THINK I'LL CALL IT CONSTANTIN–OPLE?

WHAT A CAPITAL IDEA

WHILE THE WESTERN EMPIRE GOT BATTERED BY BARBARIANS, CONSTANTINOPLE KEPT GOING FOR A THOUSAND YEARS! BUT THAT'S ANOTHER STORY...

5

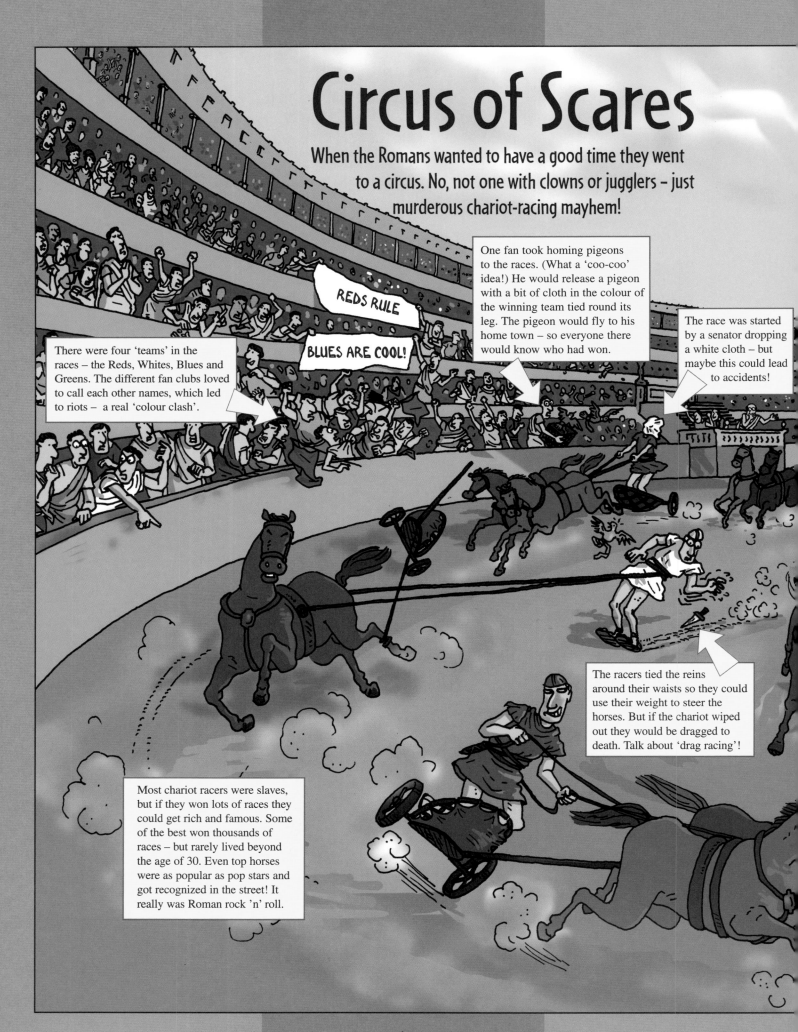

Circus of Scares

When the Romans wanted to have a good time they went to a circus. No, not one with clowns or jugglers – just murderous chariot-racing mayhem!

One fan took homing pigeons to the races. (What a 'coo-coo' idea!) He would release a pigeon with a bit of cloth in the colour of the winning team tied round its leg. The pigeon would fly to his home town – so everyone there would know who had won.

The race was started by a senator dropping a white cloth – but maybe this could lead to accidents!

REDS RULE

BLUES ARE COOL!

There were four 'teams' in the races – the Reds, Whites, Blues and Greens. The different fan clubs loved to call each other names, which led to riots – a real 'colour clash'.

The racers tied the reins around their waists so they could use their weight to steer the horses. But if the chariot wiped out they would be dragged to death. Talk about 'drag racing'!

Most chariot racers were slaves, but if they won lots of races they could get rich and famous. Some of the best won thousands of races – but rarely lived beyond the age of 30. Even top horses were as popular as pop stars and got recognized in the street! It really was Roman rock 'n' roll.

6

Want to know how many laps there are to go? Then watch the dolphins! An official would flip over a golden dolphin at the end of each lap. That way you knew how close it was to the fin-ish. (Groan!)

LAST LAP – IT'S O -FISH -AL!

HI HANDSOME, COO -EE!

The circus was extra-popular because it was one of the few times when men and women could sit together. (Shocking!)

Most chariots were drawn by four horses, but there were also races where each chariot had two. The big show-off Emperor Nero had his chariot drawn by TEN horses!

This sport could be very bad for your health. Many of the top racers got killed at the circus – in deadly chariot crashes that the Romans called 'shipwrecks'.

Want to speed up? Give your horses a whipping. Want to slow down another racer? Then give him a whipping too!

7

Play and Slay

With their gory gladiatorial games, the Romans were always game for a bit of violence. A trip to the theatre could be a real horror show, too!

The circus was certainly a thrilling bit of entertainment… if you weren't taking part. It's true to say that there was nothing the Romans liked better than a real-life drama. (They'd have loved to watch a punch-up in the playground.) But their theatre really started somewhere else...

Boogie for the gods

The Romans showed their gods how much they loved them by having chariot races in their honour at the circus. But in 360 BC a plague hit Rome – and the races didn't get rid of it. So they asked their Etruscan neighbours for help. The Etruscans sent dancers to perform in the circus. The dancing became really popular with the Romans (and with the gods too, the Romans hoped).

Play time

Around 200 BC a man called Lucius Andronicus added a story to the dancing – so it became a sort of mimed play. The idea caught on, and pretty soon the Romans had plays to watch. Lots of the play plots were pinched from the Greeks, but the Romans added their own terrible twists. They never missed a chance to act horribly, especially if the acting was horrible.

MAYBE THEY SHOULD HAVE STOPPED THE RACES BEFORE THE DANCERS CAME ON

You've watched murder stories, haven't you? But you know the blood is fake and the actors don't really get hurt. The Romans had a better idea: act out violent story and, at the last minute, put a criminal on stage and really hurt him...

Criminals were dressed in golden clothes and had to dance happily for the audience. Then suddenly they'd be set on fire and burned to death – in a 'crematio'.

The actors were often slaves, and might suffer if the audience didn't have a good time. Some even had to announce...

Lots of plays had plots as horrible as a horror film. In Seneca's play *Thyestes* for example, a father is fed a tasty stew. What he doesn't know is that it's made of his two minced kids!

I WANTED MY NAME IN LIGHTS, NOT TO BE ALIGHT – YOWCH!

IF YOU DON'T LIKE THE PLAY YOU MUST GIVE US A GOOD BEATING!

In one play the hero was acted by a criminal, and the audience watched as he had his dangly bits cut off – for real!

Sometimes this wasn't enough for the bloodthirsty Romans. The writer Terence complained that one of his plays was deserted by the spectators. They had heard there was a gladiator fight to the death in another arena, and left.

COLOSSEUM STATS

The Colosseum was an incredible place – a lot like a modern football stadium. Here are some fierce footie-fan-style facts...

- Opened in 80 AD, it held 50,000 people.
- It was actually named after a big statue (a colossus) of Nero that stood nearby.
- Its columns were supposed to be held together by iron pins but people kept nicking them, so cement was used instead.
- It was quite small compared to the Circus Maximus – which was 12 times bigger!

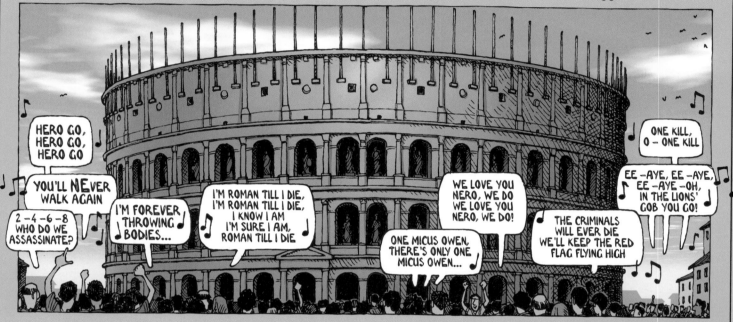

'ORRIBLY UNSAFE ARENAS

The Colosseum was fairly safe because it was built of stone. But some earlier arenas were definitely not safe. In fact they were as safe as a hedgehog on a motorway. The writer Tacitus described a terrible accident that happened because an arena was made so cheaply...

Tacitus went on to say that the dead were the lucky ones – it was worse for the mangled fans who knew their loved ones were trapped somewhere in the mess of wood and bodies. The crowds had rushed to see blood in the arena, and they certainly saw it.

Emperor Caligula did not have a big arena collapse in his time. He said...

It began and ended in a moment... Fans flocked in – men and women of all ages – because there had been very few good shows in the reign of Emperor Tiberius. The packed building collapsed, inwards and outwards, crushing or smothering a huge crowd.

WHAT A SHAME – IT MUST BE INTERESTING TO WATCH!

Not from the bottom of the heap, Cal, you crackpot!

Undressed for Success

The Olympic Games are the biggest sporting event ever. The first games were held more than 2,000 years ago, when athletes from all over ancient Greece would compete... without any clothes on!

If a sprinter wanted to get a sneaky head start, he'd better make sure he could run fast... because if he was caught, he'd get a jolly good hiding!

Boxers didn't wear gloves – they just wrapped leather strips around their hands. No wonder they ended up as ugly as old boots.

The Greeks didn't go in for fancy trainers or shirts with their sponsor's name on it. They competed completely nude!

Read everything carefully if you want to know why these women are wearing disguises!

SPLAT 'EM FOR SPARTA!

Discus-throwing could be a very big hit with the spectators...

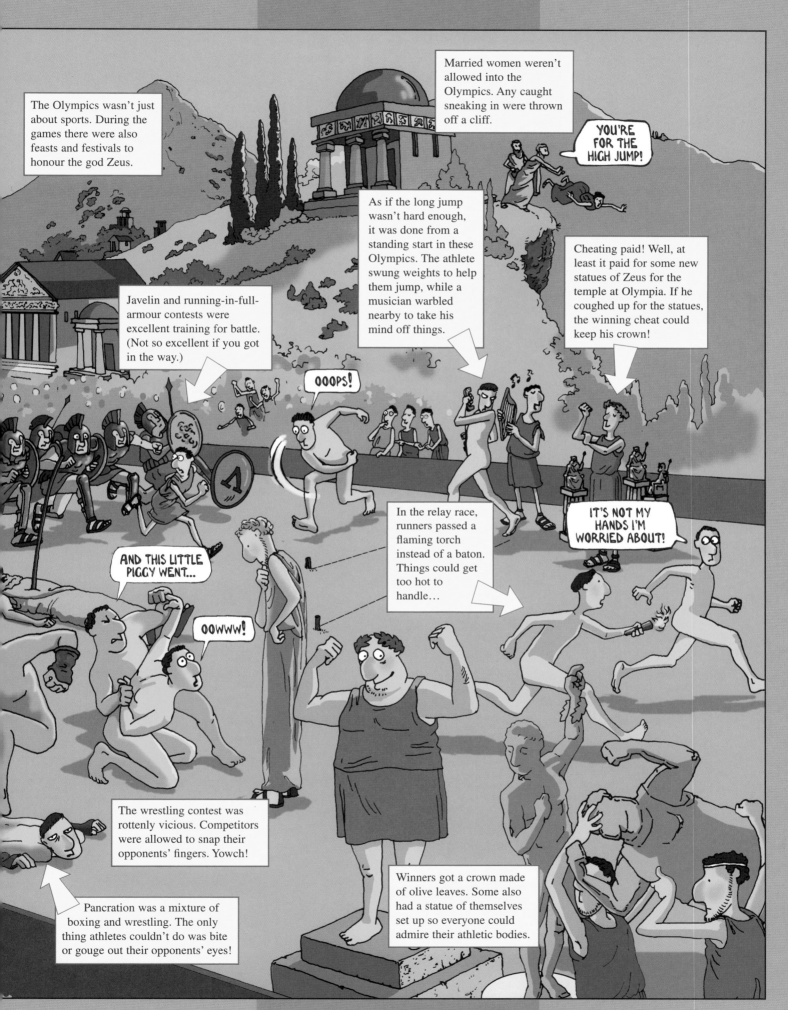

The Olympics wasn't just about sports. During the games there were also feasts and festivals to honour the god Zeus.

Married women weren't allowed into the Olympics. Any caught sneaking in were thrown off a cliff.

YOU'RE FOR THE HIGH JUMP!

As if the long jump wasn't hard enough, it was done from a standing start in these Olympics. The athlete swung weights to help them jump, while a musician warbled nearby to take his mind off things.

Cheating paid! Well, at least it paid for some new statues of Zeus for the temple at Olympia. If he coughed up for the statues, the winning cheat could keep his crown!

Javelin and running-in-full-armour contests were excellent training for battle. (Not so excellent if you got in the way.)

OOOPS!

In the relay race, runners passed a flaming torch instead of a baton. Things could get too hot to handle…

IT'S NOT MY HANDS I'M WORRIED ABOUT!

AND THIS LITTLE PIGGY WENT...

OOWWW!

The wrestling contest was rottenly vicious. Competitors were allowed to snap their opponents' fingers. Yowch!

Winners got a crown made of olive leaves. Some also had a statue of themselves set up so everyone could admire their athletic bodies.

Pancration was a mixture of boxing and wrestling. The only thing athletes couldn't do was bite or gouge out their opponents' eyes!

11

Bloody Ball Games

Roman chariot fans may have behaved like football fanatics, but, a thousand years later, actual ball games were just as bad. Take a look at this madcap medieval mob, for a start...

In Britain, the measly Middle Ages were dangerous and dismal for poor peasants. The poorer you were, the bigger the slice of tax you paid to the local lord. Laws were fouly unfair, too; common folk were bullied and beaten by barons and monks, who almost always got away with it. So... the peasants took their minds off the misery by playing gory games.

1. Mob Football

A bit like football... with no rules. You grabbed the ball and tried to get it into your opponent's goal a couple of miles away! There were any number of people on each side. Players wore normal clothes – and knives. People didn't get any red cards, but if they got stabbed, they definitely got red shirts.

2. Ice Jousting

The skates were made of animal bones strapped to the feet. Savage skaters charged at each other at speed, armed with poles. Lots of broken poles but even more broken bones. Then, of course, there was the danger of thin ice. Archaeologists dug up the skeleton of a woman from the bed of a river. Bone skates were still attached to the skeleton bones of her feet.

3. Stool Ball

A milkmaid sat on a three-legged stool. Measly men bowled a ball at her like skittles while she tried to dodge them. If they hit her then they got a prize: cakes (yum)... or cold kisses (yuck).

BEASTLY BASKETBALL

Don't get the idea that brutal ball games were only big in Europe. Far from it! Over in amazing ancient Mexico, the Aztecs played the goriest game EVER: tlatchli (say t-latch-lee). It was played in a long, thin stone court, with two teams of ten-a-side – with plenty of substitutes for players who were carried off lethally wounded... or dead. The aim was

12

SCARY SCOTTISH SOCCER

Love it or hate it, football can be as funnily foul as a clown with diarrhoea. One place where football caught on in a big and brutal way was Scotland…

Spoil sport

In 1491, James IV's parliament banned football in Scotland, because it was a waste of time… and men. The game had hardly any rules at all, and was just used as a good excuse for a punch-up.

to pass a ball through a ring set into the wall, about five metres above the ground. Sounds easy? Uh-uh. There were no rules to stop opponents killing one another. Losing was considered disgraceful, so killing the opposition was a good idea. Some historians think losing players were sacrificed to the god Xolotl. They were taken to a platform where their heads were cut off and stuck on wooden poles.

Fierce fixtures

In the 1500s, the men of the Borders played the first 'internationals' between England and Scotland. They suffered more broken legs than a centipede under a steamroller.

Queen's park

It wasn't just the common Scottish folk who liked to watch some terribly tough tackling. In 1568, Mary Queen of Scots attended a match at Carlisle between 20 of her followers and a team of English soldiers. An English reporter said the Scots had "more skillful players". What a creep!

Getting the boot

Despite joyless James, football (or 'fitba' as some tartan terrors would say) became a huge hit in Scotland. By the time of Queen Victoria, most rural folk had been forced into sorry slums and tenements in the big Scottish cities. The men unwound by – you've guessed it – playing football. One team, Queen's Park, was allowed to join the English Football Association. It was all friendly football fun with Scots footballers even playing for English clubs. But that all ended after a ferocious foul by a Queen's Park player turned into a massive fan fight – a revolting riot in fact. One of Queen's Park's defenders took the ball off the opponent's winger… and snapped the winger's leg in two. It was a (lame) leg of two halves. The fans went mad… and Scottish teams got booted out.

Highland Horrors

CAN'T WE TOSS A COIN INSTEAD?

HE'S WOLFING ME DOWN!

I'M IN NO MOO-D FOR THIS

IT'S WINNER TAKES BRAWL!

TO... HUNTERS 'N' HURLERS   TO... THE DEATH

Football matches weren't the only sporting event the Scottish split their sporrans for. You may have heard of the Highland Games, an event packed with Scotland's own national sports – some of which are truly odd and dangerous. But which of the savage sports shown here has REALLY been played in Scotland?

1) Hunt the Human

You need: One forest; servants.

How to play: Set fire to forest. Surround it with well-armed hunters. As the deer, wolves, wild boar and outlaws that live in the forest flee, kill them. Eat the deer and boar. Leave the dead outlaws for the wolves.

2) Tossing the Caber

You need: A caber (tree trunk without branches); lots of room!

How to play: Pick up trunk. Cradle one end in your hands. Toss the caber as far as you can.

3) Twisting the Legs off a Cow

You need: Dead cows – one each.

How to play: Twist off all four legs of the dead cow. The person who does it first is the winner. The prize is one fat sheep.

4) Hurley Hacket

You need: A dead horse. (There were plenty of them around in the Middle Ages!)

How to play: Boil the horse's head till all the flesh drops off. Take the skull to a hill. Use the skull as a bony sledge and slide down.

5) Gladiatorial Combat

You need: 30 men for each team, all armed with a sword, dagger, axe, crossbow with three bolts and a leather shield.

How to play: Bash, chop and bolt each other to bits. The one team with any members left alive at all wins.

Answers on page 60.

14

Dreadful James

The most hateful thing you could ever do has to be hunting and hurting people.
But one cruel king thought witch-hunting it was the best sport of all.

In slimy Stuart times, one unfair, unsporting and awful activity became all the rage: witch trials. The king, a nosepicking ninny named James I (or James VI if you're Scottish) made them really fashionable. He had some idiotic ideas about how to decide who was a witch, and he even took part in the trials himself.

Trial and horror

One thing's for sure: James was utterly convinced that witches were out to get him. Would you get a fair trial if James was there? You had more chance of seeing the Loch Ness monster on water skis. First you'd be tortured. Which terrible treatment would you prefer? Take your pick!

'PILNIEWINKS' – THUMBSCREWS TIGHTENED ON TO THE THUMBS UNTIL THEY BLEED

'CASHIELAWS' – AN IRON CASE PLACED AROUND THE LEG WHICH WAS SLOWLY HEATED

'THE BOOT' – AN IRON FOOT CRUSHER

'THE HEID ROPE' – A KNOTTED ROPE PLACED AROUND THE SKULL AND WOUND TIGHT

Stormy temper

One day James got into a serious strop when he met stormy weather while sailing into a Scottish port. So what did he do? He blamed some locals and accused them of witchcraft. The North Berwick Witches, as they became known, were arrested and tortured. Under torture they 'confessed' to…
• throwing a cat into the sea with its legs tied together with bits of a dead man. (This was supposed to be a spell to conjure up a storm!)
• breaking into a church at night with a Hand of Glory. A Hand of Glory was supposed to open locks and send people into a deep sleep. (**Note to wannabe witches**: want to make one of these? First chop off the hand of a murderer who's been hanged, then dip the hand in wax and use as a candle.)

THAT'S A HANDY CANDLE!

• making a love spell using hairs from a cow's udder. The witch's accusers even claimed the spell had backfired and the cow had fallen in love with the witch (a man).

I CAN LOVE NO UDDER

Flaming injustice

Real, made-up or downright despicably daft? Before you make up your mind, ask yourself this: was it just a coincidence that the leader of the 'witches' was James's rival to the Scottish crown? Whatever the truth, the 'witches' were burnt to death.

15

Trial and Terror

Witch trials were regularly held in Stuart villages and towns. Innocent women were put through things far scarier than anything a 'witch' could do!

'Demonology' was a book written by King James I about witches. It was used in witch trials across the land as an instruction manual on how to be beastly to women.

The poor women – and sometimes even men – who were about to stand trial for witchcraft were kept awake for days on end. This was to make sure they were so tired that they would say anything the witch finder wanted them to – including owning up to being a witch.

DEMONOLOGY

Children as young as five were called upon to tell stories about the women. The prosecutors encouraged them to make up any old nonsense... the weirder the better! Just as long as it made the women seem wicked.

Witches were supposed to keep demons or devils near them in the shape of animals – called familiars. So scram, you soppy cat – you'll be the death of her!

16

Stuart people believed that witches couldn't drown – because water rejects evil. So women were tested by being dunked underwater! If they drowned, they were probably innocent (and definitely dead!).

In Scotland, France and the rest of Europe, most women found guilty of witchcraft were burnt. However, in England most were just hanged instead.

Pricking with needles was another terrible test used by wicked witch finders. As 'witches' didn't bleed, the sneaky 'prickers' had plenty of nasty tricks up their sleeves to make sure they didn't draw blood. The poor women probably wouldn't have bled anyway as fear drains blood from the skin.

The accused was sometimes weighed against two huge Bibles. If the woman was lighter then she must be a witch! But the Bibles they used were massive! Talk about not balancing the books...

HOLY BIBLE

Witch finders would look all over women's bodies to find an odd lump or mark. Any mark would do – wart, mole, birthmark – whatever! This was supposed to be the extra nipple that witches used to feed blood to their foul familiars!

17

Which Witch?

HOW TO SPOT A WITCH...

Here are three nutty notions about witches. Which were really relied upon in Stuart times?

1 Has her next-door neighbour ever been poorly?

IT'S INFLUENZ...HER!

Whenever you're in doubt, just point the finger at someone else. They can always take the blame.

2 Has her pet ever frightened anyone?

Maybe her doggie is a being a bit too... 'familiar'. Or maybe the witch finder is a scaredy CAT.

3 If she is Scottish, does she ever answer back?

DON'T ANSWER BACK!

I DIDN'T!

AHA!!

If the answer is yes, you can accuse her of 'smeddum'. (That's Stuart speak for 'talking back'.)

FAMILIAR PROBLEM

'Familiar' was the term used for a witch's animal companion. In crackpot King James's book on the subject, which of these animals did he say could be familiars?

Answers on page 60.

18

Beastly Boney

Meet the man who was a hero to the French and a horror to everyone else – plus the men who did their best to beat him.

Napoleon Bonaparte had lots of nicknames – Boney, The Little Corporal or The Corsican Ogre, depending on whether he'd given you a medal or felled your family. Boney led thousands of young men to their deaths in war but the French still loved him. In fact, they loved him so much that they made him their emperor.

Short on luck

He was ruthless, cunning and lucky. But, of course, eventually his luck ran out. Just when Napoleon had conquered most of Europe, he threw it all away by invading Russia. Russia was too big a country just to walk in and conquer, but barmy Boney was so big-headed that he thought it would be no problem – especially as he had an army of 400,000 men. Boney got all the way to Moscow, realized it was now midwinter, and had to retreat all the way back again. Cold, disease, hunger and Russians killed 99 out of every 100 of his soldiers. And then Boney deserted his men to dash back to Paris before he was kicked out of power. Bet they didn't feel lucky.

BONEY'S BRUTAL BATTLES

In 1805 Napoleon decided to invade Britain, but the British admiral, Nelson, smashed the French forces at Trafalgar...

...SO BONEY STICKS TO LAND BATTLES – AND SMASHES THE AUSTRIANS AND RUSSIANS AT AUSTERLITZ. 26,000 MEN DIE.

THANK GOD YOU HAVE DONE YOUR DUTY

WHERE HAVE I HEARD THAT BEFORE?

1806
NAPOLEON FIGHTS THE PRUSSIANS AT JENA – BUT A BRAIN ILLNESS MEANS HE SLEEPS THROUGH THE BATTLE.

THANK GOD I HAVE DONE MY ZZZZZZZZ

1810
THE FRENCH RULE MOST OF EUROPE. NAPOLEON TELLS HIS BROTHER HIS BIG SECRET...

I reign through the fear I bring.

1812
AT BORODINO IN RUSSIA, NAPOLEON HAS A BAD BLADDER WHICH MAKES RIDING PAINFUL. STILL, HE LOOKS AT THE CORPSES AND SAYS...

It is the most beautiful battlefield I have ever seen.

1813
NAPOLEON HAS ROTTEN GUTS TOO. THEY MAKE HIM ALMOST TOO ILL TO COMMAND AT DRESDEN.

HE'S GOT A DICKY TUMMY

POOR GUY

THE FRENCH FIGHT THE RUSSIANS, PRUSSIANS, SWEDES AND AUSTRIANS AND LOSE AT LEIPZIG. 60,000 LIVES ARE LOST.

1814
NAPOLEON GIVES UP AND GOES OFF TO THE ISLAND OF ELBA. KING LOUIS XVIII (BROTHER OF CHOPPED LOUIS XVI) TAKES THE THRONE.

I GUESS YOU'RE HEAD OF THE COUNTRY NOW

I WISH YOU WOULDN'T USE THE WORD 'HEAD'

1815
NAPOLEON COMES BACK TO PARIS FOR ONE LAST TRY – BUT THEN HE MEETS THE BRITS AT WATERLOO. THE FRENCH LOSE TO THE BRITS, WHO ARE LED BY THE DUKE OF WELLINGTON.

HOW DO YOU DO?

FINE THANKS AND YOU?

1821
THE BRITS SEND NAPOLEON TO THE ISLAND OF ST HELENA. THERE IS NO ESCAPE, EXCEPT... THROUGH HIS DEATH. FAMOUS LAST WORDS?

Chief of the army!

19

Awful for Armies

Could you survive as a soldier in the time of Napoleon? An army life was awful on either side – it could kill you before you reached the battlefield!

Napoleon needed a lot of men to go around conquering. So he passed laws that said all unmarried men aged between 20 and 25 could be forced to join the army. Sometimes, the army recruiters would come to a village and hold a lottery – and the prize was… a long, hard stint in the army!

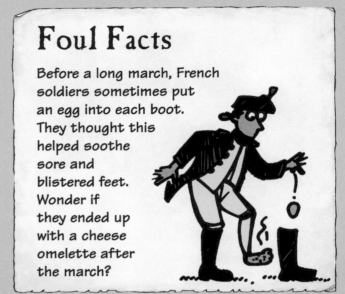

Foul Facts

Before a long march, French soldiers sometimes put an egg into each boot. They thought this helped soothe sore and blistered feet. Wonder if they ended up with a cheese omelette after the march?

CONGRATULATIONS, YOU'VE WON AN ALL-EXPENSES-PAID TRIP TO RUSSIA. MAKE SURE YOU BRING SOME WARM CLOTHES

Feet of fury

The 'lucky winners' had a time more terrible than any school trip. Napoleon marched his armies all over Europe. In fact, the soldiers could be made to march up to 40 exhausting miles every day. They were allowed five minutes rest every hour (usually to smoke a pipe), and 30 minutes rest every 18 miles. Every five days of marching, they were given a day off. Phew! You could say Napoleon insisted on blisters.

Grim grub grab

French soldiers marched with just a bag of rice and some biscuits to keep them going. Not a very exciting supper. But when you were in a war, supplies might not reach your regiment. In that case, you had to live off the land. This meant sending out search parties to find food in local farms and villages – and grab whatever they could. The starving soldiers said that they never stole food – they just found it.

FAKE TO ESCAPE

Life in the French Army was so horrid that any sensible person would try to avoid it. Choose your way out…

Fake illness Many men pretended to be sick so that the army doctors would reject them. But most doctors were wise to their tricks. You had to have a very, very good excuse!

KEEP DIGGING LADS, I'M SURE HE'S ONLY PRETENDING

BASICALLY, I'M PAYING YOU TO TAKE A HOLIDAY

GEE

Pay a pal If you had lots of money, you could pay some other idiot to take your place in the army.

Run away Many new recruits simply legged it! This was pretty risky because if you were caught you were severely punished.

WELL, HE'S CERTAINLY FIT ENOUGH FOR THE ARMY

20

Useless uniforms

If you couldn't find a way to sneak out of the army, you had to face up to your new job. The first task was to get to grips with your equipment. But some of the clothing the soldiers had to wear was useless for fighting. The British generals thought it was more important that their men looked smart than be comfortable. So they often made very smart corpses.

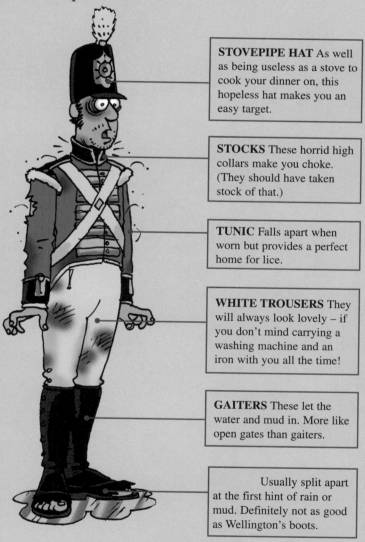

STOVEPIPE HAT As well as being useless as a stove to cook your dinner on, this hopeless hat makes you an easy target.

STOCKS These horrid high collars make you choke. (They should have taken stock of that.)

TUNIC Falls apart when worn but provides a perfect home for lice.

WHITE TROUSERS They will always look lovely – if you don't mind carrying a washing machine and an iron with you all the time!

GAITERS These let the water and mud in. More like open gates than gaiters.

Usually split apart at the first hint of rain or mud. Definitely not as good as Wellington's boots.

Drudgery and trudgery

The British Army prided itself on its strict training regime – two to three hours every day for six months. "Hah, easy!" you say, "they should try school." Some of the training involved target practice, but most of the time new recruits practised marching… and more marching… and then marching some more. This was enough to make you as mad as a March hare.

Drum roll up

When a British regiment needed more men, it sent drummers into a town or the countryside to bash their drums. If you heard the drums and needed a job so badly that you were prepared to join the army, you knew which way to go. (That's why we still use the expression 'drumming up support'.) If you weren't that daft, you knew which direction to run away from!

Grotty grub

British soldiers' food was grim, but you were glad to get it – even if it was the same every day. You might think school dinners are bad, but wait until you see these rotten rations…

- A lump of hard bread or biscuit. Be careful not to break your teeth!
- Beef (mostly bone).
- A small cup of dried peas.
- A small piece of hard cheese – so hard that even mice would turn their noses up at it!
- Rice – with added beetles.

WE'VE 'AD THE RICE, LET'S TAKE THE BISCUIT

BED BUGS

The Napoleonic Wars didn't just happen in Europe. Between 1793 and 1801, 45,000 British soldiers died in the West Indies. But only about 4,500 died through fighting. Perhaps another 500 died in accidents or because of punishments. So how did the other 40,000 die? Through disease. Cramped in hot and steamy barracks, with bad food to eat, the soldiers soon passed on deadly dysentery to each other or caught malaria. There were very few medicines so if you caught a dire disease you usually died.

PSST! I'VE GOT DYSENTERY, PASS IT ON!

21

Snow Way Home

Napoleon's troops and followers had a terrible time when they had to retreat in Russia. It was a sorry tale of snow and woe.

MMM... COOL JACKET

Many of Napoleon's men froze to death because they didn't have thick coats or boots – so soldiers were quick to nick clothes from their dead comrades.

GIVE US A HAND, MATE

I CAN'T. MINE HAVE FROZEN!

Money was worthless to a soldier when he was starving. Soldiers ended up having bust ups over bits of baguettes!

When awful army rations ran out, soldiers starved – unless they weren't fussy about what they ate. In Russia, French soldiers ate their horses – and then ate dead pals. Troop soup!

PIERRE WAS A LOUSY COOK

BUT HE MAKES A TASTY STEW!

22

Horses got hungry too. If they couldn't find hay to munch on, then a thatched roof would have to do.

Any soldier who strayed from the main retreat was cut down by cruel Cossacks (Russian horsemen).

I LIKE TO THINK OF THEM AS PETS

The soldiers at the back kept on fighting – and dying.

Soldiers were so cold that some even used the still-warm bodies of dead horses as sleeping bags!

I PREFER ICE TO LICE

YOU WON'T FEEL THE COLD ANYMORE

Most soldiers became infested with lice – itchy insects that drink human blood. Some soldiers got so sick of feeling lousy and itchy with lice that they burnt their clothes – even if it meant freezing to death.

23

Play 'Napoleon's Luck'!

Here's a game for two or more – fight Boney's battles to win a war! All you need is a dice and some counters – pennies will do. First one to throw a six starts...

STOP HERE!
To win the game you must fight the Battle of Waterloo. Throw: 1 – You lose the battle. You are captured and sent to the Island of St Helena. You're out. 2-4 – You lose... but escape. Go back six. 5-6 – You win! Move on one and shout "I am the Emperor of Europe!"

FINISH

You are sent to prison on the Isle of Elba. Move back four.

You become consul (a ruler of France). Throw again.

Nelson destroys your fleet in the Battle of the Nile. Retreat three places.

YOU'RE A LITTLE ANNOYING

You win the Battle of Marengo. Move on two.

WHAT'S UP DEAR?

Your army is forced to retreat from Moscow and is destroyed. Go back eight.

You crown yourself Emperor. Salute the crowds – and move on three.

HOORAY FOR ME!

Marie-Louise of Austria doesn't like you. Have a sulk and miss a go.

You win the Battle of the Pyramids. Move on one.

You win the Battle of Borodino, but it feels like a defeat. Trudge forward two.

Nelson sinks your fleet at Trafalgar. Go back three and miss a go.

You marry Marie-Louise of Austria – smart move. Move on one.

I'M SUNK

You win the Battle of Austerlitz. Throw again.

You win the Battle of Rivoli. Move on one.

HERE'S YOUR SPECIAL SOFT PILLOW, SIR

OWCH!

You have a painful bottom. Stand up while you miss two goes!

You decide to invade Russia. Are you sure? Miss a go for being foolish.

You win the Battle of Wagram. Advance one.

You are promoted to general. Take a bow, General Napoleon.

LET ME OUT!

START

You are jailed for being a rebel. Throw 5 or 6 to escape and then move two. 1-4, miss a go and try again.

You use cannons to break up a mob in Paris. Nasty work, Nap! Move on two.

24

Terrible Travellers

If sport bores you and the idea of being a soldier appalls you, why
not try another way of travelling the world and ruining things?
No, not being a tourist – become an explorer!

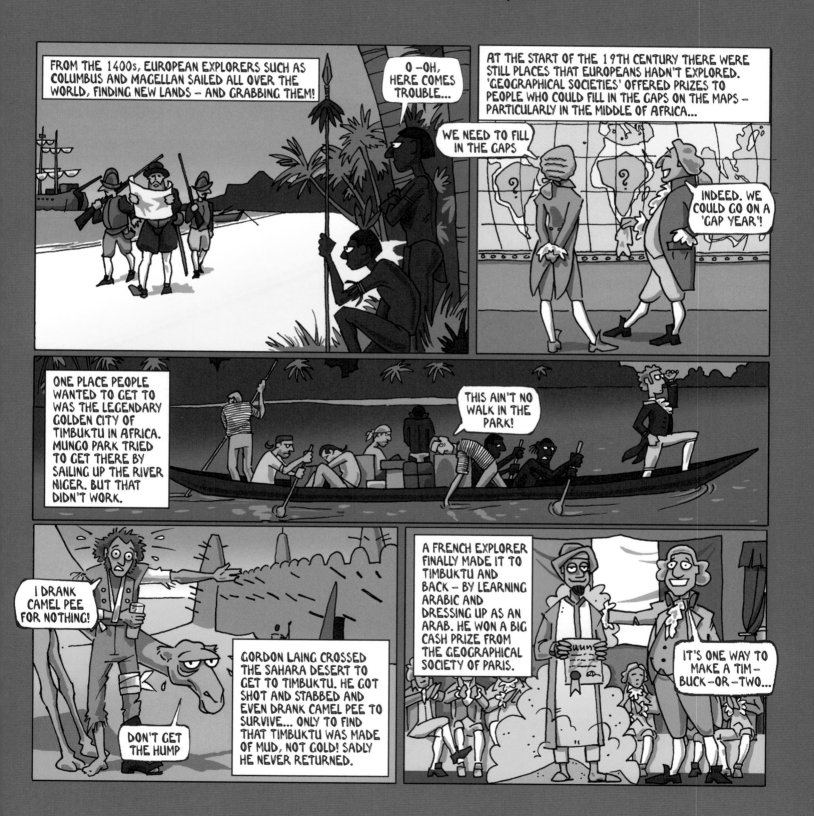

FROM THE 1400s, EUROPEAN EXPLORERS SUCH AS COLUMBUS AND MAGELLAN SAILED ALL OVER THE WORLD, FINDING NEW LANDS – AND GRABBING THEM!

O –OH, HERE COMES TROUBLE...

AT THE START OF THE 19TH CENTURY THERE WERE STILL PLACES THAT EUROPEANS HADN'T EXPLORED. 'GEOGRAPHICAL SOCIETIES' OFFERED PRIZES TO PEOPLE WHO COULD FILL IN THE GAPS ON THE MAPS – PARTICULARLY IN THE MIDDLE OF AFRICA...

WE NEED TO FILL IN THE GAPS

INDEED. WE COULD GO ON A 'GAP YEAR'!

ONE PLACE PEOPLE WANTED TO GET TO WAS THE LEGENDARY GOLDEN CITY OF TIMBUKTU IN AFRICA. MUNGO PARK TRIED TO GET THERE BY SAILING UP THE RIVER NIGER. BUT THAT DIDN'T WORK.

THIS AIN'T NO WALK IN THE PARK!

I DRANK CAMEL PEE FOR NOTHING!

DON'T GET THE HUMP

GORDON LAING CROSSED THE SAHARA DESERT TO GET TO TIMBUKTU. HE GOT SHOT AND STABBED AND EVEN DRANK CAMEL PEE TO SURVIVE... ONLY TO FIND THAT TIMBUKTU WAS MADE OF MUD, NOT GOLD! SADLY HE NEVER RETURNED.

A FRENCH EXPLORER FINALLY MADE IT TO TIMBUKTU AND BACK – BY LEARNING ARABIC AND DRESSING UP AS AN ARAB. HE WON A BIG CASH PRIZE FROM THE GEOGRAPHICAL SOCIETY OF PARIS.

IT'S ONE WAY TO MAKE A TIM – BUCK –OR –TWO...

25

NOT EVERYONE WAS IN IT FOR THE MONEY. SCOTTISH DOCTOR DAVID LIVINGSTONE WENT TO AFRICA TO TEACH ABOUT CHRISTIANITY – BUT THE AFRICANS WEREN'T INTERESTED.

WOULD YOU LIKE TO HEAR ABOUT MY GOD?

NO THANKS, WE'VE GOT LOTS ALREADY

THE NEXT THING PEOPLE WANTED TO DISCOVER WAS THE 'SOURCE OF THE NILE'*. EXPLORERS BURTON AND SPEKE SET OFF TO FIND IT...

GOSH, THESE GUYS MUST REALLY LIKE SAUCE!

*THE PLACE WHERE THE RIVER BEGAN.

BOTH OF THEM GOT SICK. BURTON STOPPED, BUT SPEKE KEPT GOING. HE FOUND THE 'SOURCE' – A BIG LAKE WHICH HE NAMED AFTER THE QUEEN. IT WAS THE PEAK OF SPEKE'S CAREER.

I NAME THIS LAKE VICTORIA!

WHO'S THIS 'VICTORIA' ANYWAY?

DUNNO. HIS GIRLFRIEND?

LIVINGSTONE ALSO TRIED TO FIND THE SOURCE OF THE NILE, BUT GOT LOST. HE WAS FOUND BY HENRY MORTON STANLEY – A NEWSPAPER REPORTER WHO WANTED A STORY.

YOU CAN'T ESCAPE THESE REPORTERS ANYWHERE!

STANLEY LATER EXPLORED THE CONGO. HE HELPED KING LEOPOLD OF BELGIUM TAKE IT OVER AND ENSLAVE ITS PEOPLE.

THESE REPORTERS REALLY ARE BAD NEWS!

STANLEY TAKES CONGO... Stanley has swept across the Congo, beating the natives into submission and taming yet another African state by sheer

IN EGYPT, EXPLORERS WERE BUSY DIGGING UP THE COUNTRY'S PAST. SOME (LIKE CIRCUS STRONGMAN GIOVANNI BELZONI) JUST WANTED TO FIND ANCIENT TREASURES AND SELL THEM.

THAT'S NOT FAIR TRADE

FOR SALE

NO, IT'S PHARAOH TRADE!

26

MEANWHILE, A DARING DUO CALLED LEWIS AND CLARK MADE THE FIRST JOURNEY RIGHT ACROSS NORTH AMERICA AND BACK – HELPED ON THEIR WAY BY FRIENDLY INDIANS...

THE SOONER WE GET THEM OUT OF HERE, THE BETTER FOR US

UNFORTUNATELY FOR THE LOCALS, WHERE THE EXPLORERS WENT, SETTLERS AND COLONISTS FOLLOWED...

WE'RE MOVING IN – IF THAT'S OK WITH YOU...

ANOTHER BIG BLANK BIT ON THE MAPS WAS THE MIDDLE OF AUSTRALIA. CLUELESS EXPLORERS BURKE AND WILLS CAME A CROPPER WHEN TRYING TO CROSS THE CONTINENT ON CAMELS...

IS IT TOO LATE TO BACK OUT OF THE OUTBACK?

THE NORTH AND SOUTH POLES WERE ALSO UNKNOWN – AND DOZENS DIED TRYING TO EXPLORE THEM TOO.

ICY DEAD PEOPLE!

BY THE BEGINNING OF THE 20TH CENTURY, NEW INVENTIONS SUCH AS THE PLANE AND THE CAR HAD MADE EXPLORING MUCH EASIER. SOON MOST OF THE WORLD WAS MAPPED. (BUT THAT'S NOT TO SAY THAT EXPLORING IS ALL OVER. THERE ARE STILL NEW FRONTIERS TO BE EXPLORED. AS WELL AS OUTER SPACE, THERE'S A HUGE PART OF THE EARTH WE REALLY DON'T KNOW MUCH ABOUT – THE DEPTHS OF THE OCEANS.

GOSH, WHAT A HIDEOUS CREATURE!

GOSH, WHAT A HIDEOUS CREATURE!

27

Arctic Terror

In 1845, Franklin set off to find a sea route along the coast of North America that would link the Atlantic and Pacific oceans – the Northwest Passage. He had two ships and 128 men... who all ended up frozen stiff(s)!

WHAT A BUNCH OF WALLIES

AT LEAST WE'LL BE ABLE TO WRITE HOME...

TONK!

YIKES – KILLER ICICLES!

...MY PANTS ARE FULL OF LICE!

...FULL OF LOVELY USELESS STUFF...

WE MAY HAVE NO TEA BUT AT LEAST WE HAVE LOVELY CUPS TO NOT DRINK IT FROM!

SLIDE, SLIDE, SLIDE YOUR BOAT...

...RIGHT ACROSS THE ICE...

FLIP!

28

TRAGIC TRUDGE

1. Franklin's ships, the HMS *Erebus* and HMS *Terror*, made it to the Arctic, but then they got stuck in the ice – for a terrible TWO YEARS! During this time Franklin and 23 other men died from scurvy. The ice crushed the ships like matchsticks, so the survivors just had to abandon ships and walk away, dragging their stuff behind them.

2. They loaded up sleds and a lifeboat – with absolutely useless stuff: organs, posh tableware, mahogany writing desks, books, and slippers!

3. The local Inuits weren't so silly. They picked off all the useful stuff – ropes, wood and fuel.

4. Lumbered with daft gear and dressed in flimsy clothes, the crackpot crew struggled to survive.

5. The plan was to trudge to Canada. But the way was full of thin ice and killer crevasses.

6. They just made it to the land. There was still some tinned food, but the men were getting iller…

7. They ate seal livers (7A). (Too many of which are poisonous, as you and all Inuits know.) They tried rotten reindeer too (7B).

8. Then they ate their clothes. (Bet they tasted pants.)

9. Some people think the crew then ate each other… until there was no one left.

10. In 1847, one of the men left a note in a stone pile telling about their frosty fate. Then he died.

29

Dress to Empress

This handsome chap wants to wear only things that British explorers really wore when Queen Victoria ruled the British Empire – the largest empire the world has ever seen.
So help him out – which of these are real and which are bogus?

SCHOOL CAP
It's the perfect thing for that geography field trip to find the source of the Limpopo River!

BUS CONDUCTOR CAP
Ding ding! Last stop, Timbuktu!

HURRY UP, I'M CATCHING A CHILL

BIG BEARD
No comb, no razor, no barber? No problem! Nothing impresses the native ladies like big bushy face fur.

'DEERSTALKER' HAT
What's on, Watson? Why, the very same hat worn by Sherlock Holmes, that's what. Ideal wear for solving the mystery of the lost city.

WOOLLEN KILT
Trousers can get very hot and sweaty in the tropics. A kilt is better for keeping your dangly bits air-conditioned.

Y-FRONTS
Why not? A pair of these practical cotton undies is a must!

DRESS (WITH PETTICOATS)
Just because you're in Africa doesn't mean you have to be out of fashion! This swish item means you're ladylike even in 'the Dark Continent' (Africa).

Answer on page 60.

30

Way Out West!

Help Lewis and Clark lead their Corps (say core) of Discovery across North America.
Will you head home as heroes or die in Missouri misery?
To play, two or more players need a dice and some counters (pennies will do).

You meet Shoshone Indians. Chief turns out to be Sacagawea's brother. Result! Roll again.

You have to carry your boats up the mountain. Miss two goes.

Chased up tree by giant grizzly bear. Miss a turn while you wait for it to go away.

Oops, you pick wrong fork of Missouri. Downriver you go!

No food left. You're hungry enough to eat a horse, so you do. Yuk, miss a go.

Reached the Great Falls. Some horses slip and have a great fall. Roll dice. 5-6 – you find the super shortcut upriver.

Help Mandan Indians by chopping off a kid's toe without anaesthetic! (It was frostbitten.)

Buy meat from some Indian chums. Turns out to be dog! Dog-licious.

FIDO

Hire Sacagawea, brilliant Shoshone Indian girl guide. Roll again.

Blown back one space by scary storm.

Teton Indians try to grab a boat. Roll dice. 1-3 – fight, miss a go. 4-6 – make peace, carry on.

Reach the Pacific. Hooray, terrific.

Which way home? Let women and slaves vote – first time in US. Roll a dice. 1-2 – oops, wrong choice, go all way back downstream.

Playing 'it' with friendly Nez Perce Indians. 'It's' fun. Move on two.

Wrap new baby in flag and make friends with Sioux (say 'Sue') Indians. Move on one.

Sergeant Floyd is the first of the Corps to become a corpse. Bury body and miss a turn.

Blackfoot Indians put boot into you. It's not fun. Move back two.

Almost home. Fancy going round again for an 'en-Corps'?

FINISH

START

31

Up the Creek

With their lack of bush skills, Burke and Wills' Australian walkabout was woeful. Things got even worse when they went up Cooper's Creek...

OH NO! HE'S GONE BURKO!

I'M FED UP

I'M STARVING

RATS

DIG 3 FT NW APR 21 1861

32

AN EXPLORER'S GUIDE TO AWFUL EATING OUT

1. The doomed duo missed a helper who was supposed to meet them at the creek. Before he went, he buried some food and carved directions to it on a tree. Burke, Wills and King dug it up – and ate it all.
2. Cooper's Creek wasn't short of food if you knew where to look. Burke didn't.
3. Burke hated relying on Aboriginals. He refused to their fish. What a wally.
4. Soon they had nothing to munch on apart from rat kebabs (yuck)…
5. …and the nardoo plant. Not poisonous if you prepare it properly. They didn't.
6. How were buckets, enema syringes (for squirting water up their bums) and 80 pairs of shoes going to help them now?
7. The camels had turned nasty. One bit a bit out of a trekker's bum!
8. They left the creek to search of Mount Hopeless, but failed to find it and walked around in circles. That just about sums them up – hopeless.

CAMELS GET THE HUMP TOO, YOU KNOW

I SWEAR THAT CAMEL'S NEXT

IT'S NOT SURPRISING WE'VE BEEN GOING IN CIRCLES – THE SHOES ARE ALL LEFT FOOTERS!

FIDDLESTICKS!

£2,000 Grand Prize

33

Bad for Beggars

Those explorers were posh or potty enough to be able to make a choice about their lives.
Back in Victorian Britain, beggars couldn't be choosers. They could be cheeky and sneaky, though...

Do you ever get fed up with being treated like a kid? Want to be treated like a grown-up? Not if you were a Victorian kid you wouldn't. Because Victorian children could be punished like adults! One ten-year-old boy told his story to a reporter…

THE BEGGAR'S TALE

I was born in Wisbech near Cambridge. My mother died when I was five and my father married again. My stepmother hated me so I ran away.

I lived by begging and sleeping rough and made my way to London. There I'd sleep on doorsteps or anywhere that gave a little shelter.

I suffered terribly from hunger and at times I thought I'd starve. I got crusts but I can hardly tell how I lived.

One night I was sleeping under a railway bridge when a policeman came along and asked me what I was up to. I said I had no place to go and he said I had to go with him.

The next morning he took me to court and told the judge there were always lots of boys living under the bridge. They were young thieves and they gave a lot of trouble. I was mixing with them so I was given 14 days in prison.

I'll carry on begging and go from workhouse to workhouse to sleep. I am unhappy but I have to get used to it.

We don't know what happened to this boy. Did he ever find happiness? Did anyone care?

Some boys went pick-pocketing and weren't bothered if they were caught. If they were sent to prison then at least they were given food and shelter.

Child cheats

Want to make some dishonest money? Here are some tips from villainous Victorian children you must NOT try at home…

1. THE SHIVERING DODGE

The shivering dodge was a favourite of 'Shaking Jemmy'. He shivered so long he couldn't stop – even when he was in the warm.

There was another fake shake – the 'shakelurk', which meant pretending you'd been shipwrecked.

2. THE LUCIFER DODGE

You can get your little friends to gather up the matches and try it again... and again... and again. Hopefully no one will 'catch' on.

3. THE TEA AND SUGAR DODGE

The empty packets were called a 'fakement' – a thing used to make your story believable. A bit like a sick note you've written yourself. (You'd never do that though, would you?!)

This dodge could earn up to 18 shillings in one morning. Doesn't sound much, but at this time many working men didn't make ten shillings a week. Now that's criminal.

4. THE SCALDRUM DODGE

If looking burnt, blistered or lame doesn't help then pretend to choke on a piece of dry bread. Take money to get ale to wash the dry bread from your throat.

If everything else fails then try this really disgusting way of getting some gross grub…

5. THE BIRD-BREAD DODGE

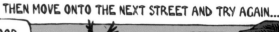

Top tip for starving street folk: it is best if the bread is covered in maggots. Do NOT shake them off before you eat the bread – they make a nice bit of meat in your sandwich.

MUM'S THE WORST!

Of course beggars and thieves got caught – and punished. A child was taken to a court in Birmingham. He was a thief. The judge said to the child's mother…

Would your mother rather see you in prison than take you home ? (Better not ask just in case she says "Yes"!) The judge had the boy sent to a prison hulk (a ship). The boy was too young to take care of himself and died. He was six years and seven months old. A young Victorian who got what he deserved? No. A villainous Victorian victim.

35

Rotten Riverside

These poor Victorians are 'going with the flow' – grubbing in the muck of the River Thames. (Oh... and can you spot seven terrible Thamesside top hats in this picture?)

The 'mudlarks' (poor kids who grubbed in the mud for scrap) had to work even in the middle of winter. They could only warm up by standing in the warm waste water from factories.

The 'dredgermen' fished in the river. Of course, the water was so stinky that no fish could live in it. So the dredgers fished for lumps of coal – and anything else that fell off ships!

HEADS!

YOU SHOULD HAVE SEEN THE ONE THAT GOT AWAY!

WHAT A CATCH

Finding a bloated body was a bit of a bonus! The dredgers could clean out its pockets – then hand the body over to the authorities for a reward.

36

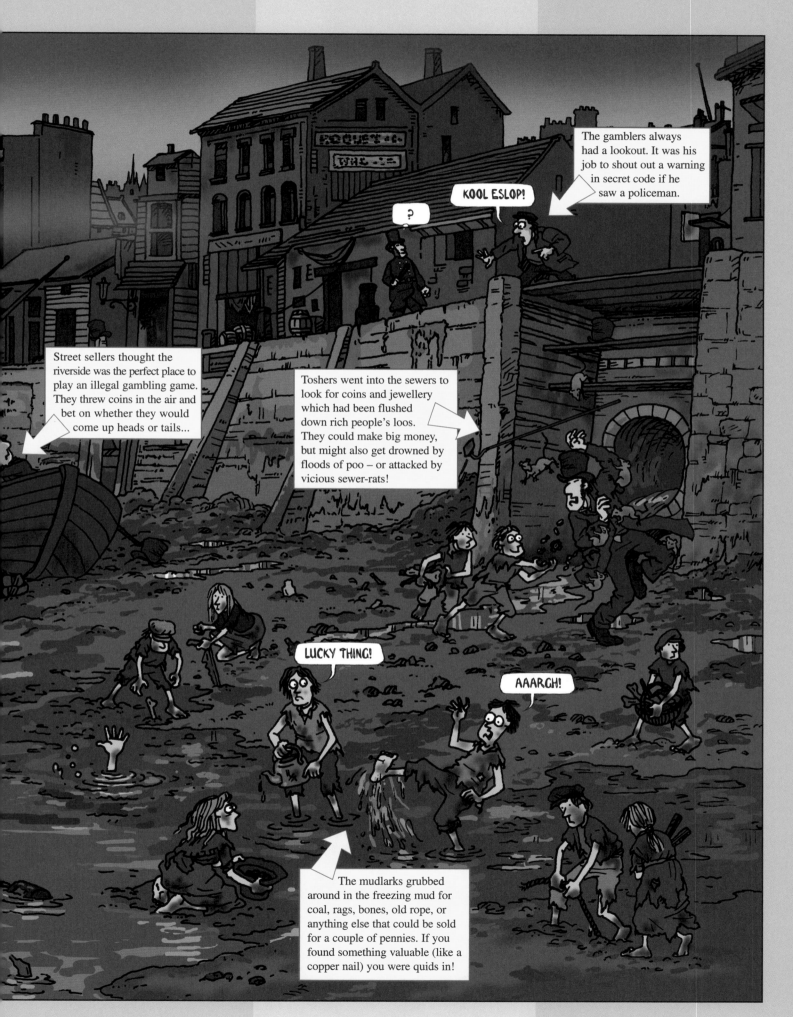

The gamblers always had a lookout. It was his job to shout out a warning in secret code if he saw a policeman.

KOOL ESLOP!

?

Street sellers thought the riverside was the perfect place to play an illegal gambling game. They threw coins in the air and bet on whether they would come up heads or tails...

Toshers went into the sewers to look for coins and jewellery which had been flushed down rich people's loos. They could make big money, but might also get drowned by floods of poo – or attacked by vicious sewer-rats!

LUCKY THING!

AAARGH!

The mudlarks grubbed around in the freezing mud for coal, rags, bones, old rope, or anything else that could be sold for a couple of pennies. If you found something valuable (like a copper nail) you were quids in!

37

Answers on page 60-61.

Cruel Schools

Which punishment did the Victorians give us? The rack? A whack?
No – having to go to school, of course!

The Industrial Schools Act of 1857 let judges send children from 7 to 14 to 'industrial schools' where they would be taught reading and writing, and learn useful skills like sewing and woodwork.

Little Devils

In 1857 a new law was passed. It came up with a new way of punishing little criminals who committed little crimes. What was this punishment?

a) Little devils were whipped ten times with a leather belt.

b) Little devils were sent to school.

c) Little devils were fastened in stocks and pelted with hot cabbage.

d) Little devils had their little fingers cut off.

The answer is b).

CUT OFF MY FINGERS? PHEW! FOR A MINUTE THERE I THOUGHT YOU WERE GOING TO SEND ME TO SCHOOL

In 1861 the law said the industrial schools should be used for any child…

• under 14, caught begging
• found wandering homeless
• found with a gang of thieves
• under 12 who has committed a crime
• under 14 whose parents say they are out of control.

See that last one?

YOU CAN SEE FOR YOURSELF, OFFICER, SHE'S COMPLETELY OUT OF CONTROL

That's probably why YOU'VE been sentenced to school.

And industrial schools were even worse than the ones you have to go to. Children worked from six in the morning till seven at night. You'd be too tired to go 'out of control' after that.

I WANT YOU TO WRITE A STORY CALLED 'WHAT I DID IN MY HOLIDAYS'

PLEASE SIR, YOU HAVEN'T LEARNED ME HOW TO WRITE YET

NO, NO! YOU HAVEN'T TAUGHT ME HOW TO WRITE YET

I THOUGHT YOU WAS SUPPOSED TO LEARN ME

ONLY SEVEN HOURS TO GO

Crime School

In 1870 a new law said that there had to be schools for everyone. This took criminal kids off the streets and into criminal classrooms instead.

KNOCKY-NINE-DOORS

There's a game that has been played ever since doors were invented. But in the 1850s it was against the law, and children who were caught could go to prison...

WE HAVE THIS GAME OF KNOCKING ON DOORS AND RUNNING AWAY. WE TRY TO DO NINE DOORS WITHOUT GETTING CAUGHT. IT'S CALLED 'KNOCKY-NINE-DOORS'

COME TO... CRIMINAL CLASSES!

The kids in the new classes learned Maths and English and so on — but they did not learn speaking and listening skills like they do in British schools today. What a shame! Imagine some of the true stories those criminal kids could have told...

LAST NIGHT ME AND ME SISTER WENT OUT SINGING TO MAKE SOME MONEY. WE TOOK OUR BABY BROTHER SO PEOPLE WOULD FEEL SORRY FOR US — HE'S TWO YEARS OLD. WE HAD TO STICK PINS IN HIM TO MAKE HIM CRY. YOU SHOULD HAVE HEARD HIM YELL

This happened in London in 1848 — but it could have happened at almost any time, any place, in Victoria's vile Britain.

MY DAD CAME HOME DRUNK ONE NIGHT AND SAID HE WAS GOING TO DROWN ME AND MY BROTHER. HE TOLD OUR STEP-MOTHER TO FETCH OUR SHOES. SHE JUST SAID, "IF YOU'RE GOING TO DROWN THEM YOU MIGHT AS WELL LEAVE THE SHOES FOR ME TO SELL." HE TOOK US AND THREW ME IN. I WAS ONLY SAVED BY A BOATMAN THAT FISHED ME OUT

In 1853 this really happened. Many parents dropped unwanted babies into canals in Victorian times, but it was not so common for them to try to kill off grown boys!

ME AND MY FRIENDS START A FIGHT OUTSIDE A SHOP AND MAYBE BUMP AGAINST THE WINDOW. WHEN THE SHOPKEEPER COMES OUT TO SORT US OUT, ONE OF THE LADS NIPS IN AND ROBS HIS TILL

Children as young as six years old were up to this trick. Sometimes they used girls to get the shopkeeper's mind off his till by talking to him. They thought shopkeepers would trust girls more than boys. Hmm.

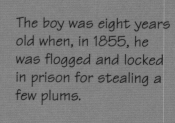

SORRY I MISSED SCHOOL FOR THE LAST FORTNIGHT, SIR, BUT I WAS IN PRISON. I GOT FOURTEEN DAYS AND A FLOGGING FOR THEFT BECAUSE I STOLE SIX PLUMS FROM A RICH WOMAN'S GARDEN

The boy was eight years old when, in 1855, he was flogged and locked in prison for stealing a few plums.

Street Strife

OI, ONE-EYED BUFFER, WHERE'S DRUNKEN BET?

WITH DAFT DARREN

STOP ALL THAT YELLIN' ROTTEN HERRINGS

DIRTY SALLY! LOOK AT DANCING SUE AND SPUDDY

SHUT YER TRAP, SMELLY SHARON!

MORNIN', JAW BREAKER

GET LOST, PINEAPPLE JACK!

'COSTER' THAT!

One lousy lifestyle you could have in Victorian times was being a street trader – a Coster. Costers were tough types, and had lots of nutty nicknames for each other. Here are ten – but two have been made up. Can you spot which two are the phoneys?

CRIME FINES

Victorian punishments could be harsh even if the villain was a child. If you were lucky, though, you'd just be fined. Some of these are crimes that carried a fine, some aren't. Can you spot the fakes?

1. Racing your dogs along the street (and betting on the winner).
2. Being cheeky to a teacher.
3. Snowballing.
4. Forgetting to do your homework.
5. Sliding on the pavement.
6. Eating a pork pie after 9pm.
7. Being a man but dressing in women's clothing.
8. Laughing in school.
9. Shaking a carpet in the street after 9am.
10. Sticking your tongue out at a teacher.
11. Dumping your dead cat in the road.
12. Coughing in church.
13. Throwing orange peel on the pavement.

IT'S A FAIR COP. I WAS A BIT RUSHED WITH MY MAKE-UP THIS MORNING. WAS IT MY LIP-LINER THAT GAVE ME AWAY?

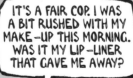

Answers on page 61.

40

Russian Riot

The Russian people suffered for years under their terrible ruler, Tsar Nicholas II.
When they decided they couldn't take it anymore, it was time for revolution!
One gang of bossyboots decided the people needed to be led – or dead!

AT THE START OF THE 20TH CENTURY, NICHOLAS II HAD ALL THE POWER. IF PEASANTS PROTESTED, THEY WOULD GET KILLED BY HIS ARMY.

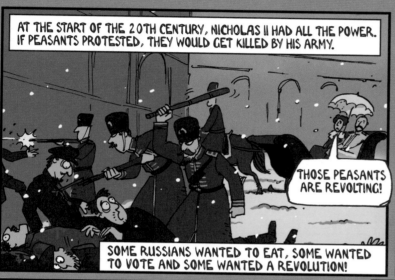

THOSE PEASANTS ARE REVOLTING!

SOME RUSSIANS WANTED TO EAT, SOME WANTED TO VOTE AND SOME WANTED A REVOLUTION!

THE BOLSHEVIKS WERE ONE GANG OF REVOLUTIONARIES. THEY BELIEVED THAT THE TSAR SHOULD BE KICKED OUT AND THAT WORKERS SHOULD TAKE CONTROL OF THE COUNTRY.

WE MUST GET RID OF THE TSAR!

UM, GENTLEMEN? THE TSAR'S SECRET POLICE WOULD LIKE A WORD WITH YOU...

LENIN (THE LEADER)

TROTSKY* (THE ARMY EXPERT)

STALIN (WHO DID THE BORING PAPERWORK)

* TROTSKY WASN'T A BOLSHEVIK AT FIRST – HE JOINED THEM LATER.

THE TSAR SENT TROUBLEMAKERS TO HORRIBLE PRISON CAMPS. THE BOLSHEVIK LEADERS WERE SENT THERE LOADS OF TIMES, BUT ALWAYS ESCAPED.

YOU IDIOT! THEY SAID THEY WERE JUST POPPING OUT FOR ICE CREAM, AND YOU BELIEVED THEM – AGAIN!?

IN 1905, A GROUP OF STARVING WORKERS MARCHED TO THE TSAR'S PALACE. THEY SAID THAT THEY WERE SO HUNGRY THAT THEY MIGHT AS WELL DIE, AND ASKED THE TSAR FOR HELP.

YOU WANT TO DIE? VERY WELL – FIRE!

THE TSAR'S TROOPS SHOT THEM. THIS MASSACRE MADE PEOPLE SO ANGRY THAT RIOTS BROKE OUT ALL OVER RUSSIA.

THE ONLY WAY THE TSAR COULD STOP THE RIOTS WAS BY MAKING A PARLIAMENT OR 'DUMA' THAT PEOPLE COULD VOTE FOR. BUT THEN THE TSAR IGNORED THE DUMA – WHICH WAS PRETTY DUMB!

IT'S A CASE OF DUMB AND DUMA!

WHAT DID I DO?

IN 1914, THE FIRST WORLD WAR STARTED. RUSSIA ENDED UP FIGHTING AGAINST GERMANY AND AUSTRIA–HUNGARY. THE RUSSIAN ARMY WAS HUGE, BUT MANY SOLDIERS HAD NO RIFLES OR BOOTS. MILLIONS WERE SLAUGHTERED.

THESE RUSSIAN FOOT SOLDIERS ARE MOSTLY 'ARMLESS!

41

THE WAR MADE THINGS EVEN WORSE IN RUSSIA — THERE WAS LITTLE FOOD AND PEOPLE GOT EVEN ANGRIER. IN 1917, PEOPLE ALL OVER RUSSIA REBELLED AGAINST THE TSAR IN THE 'FEBRUARY REVOLUTION'. THE ARMY WAS TOLD TO SHOOT THE REBELS, BUT LOTS OF SOLDIERS DECIDED TO SHOOT THEIR OFFICERS INSTEAD!

DOWN WITH THE TSAR!

IF YOU INSIST...

FIRE!

AT THIS TIME, THE BOLSHEVIKS WERE TRYING TO CONVINCE PEOPLE THAT THEY SHOULD BE RUNNING THE COUNTRY. THEY SET UP WORKERS' COUNCILS (SOVIETS) AND EVEN A WORKERS' ARMY (THE RED GUARD).

SUPPORT US AND YOU WILL GET LAND, BREAD AND PEACE!

BUT I DON'T LIKE PEAS

IN MARCH 1917, THE PROTESTS GOT SO BAD THAT NICHOLAS QUIT AS TSAR. THE BOLSHEVIKS AND THE DUMA AGREED TO SHARE POWER.

YEAH, RIGHT!

SHARE AND SHARE ALIKE, RIGHT COMRADE?

BUT THE BOLSHEVIKS DIDN'T WANT TO SHARE POWER! IN OCTOBER 1917, THEIR RED GUARDS 'HEROICALLY' TOOK OVER THE WINTER PALACE, THE BUILDING WHERE THE GOVERNMENT WAS BASED. IT HELPED THAT NO ONE TRIED TO STOP THEM...

EXCUSE ME, WE'VE COME TO STORM THE WINTER PALACE. COULD YOU LET US IN?

OH, ALL RIGHT THEN...

LENIN ALSO MADE PEACE WITH GERMANY AND PULLED OUT OF THE FIRST WORLD WAR.

BUT SOME SNOOTY RUSSIANS WANTED THE TSAR BACK. THEY GOT TOGETHER TO FORM THE 'WHITE ARMY' AND BATTLE THE BOLSHEVIKS — SO TROTSKY FORMED THE RED GUARDS INTO AN ARMY TO FIGHT THEM BACK. RUSSIA HAD ONLY JUST GOT OUT OF THE FOUL FIRST WORLD WAR — NOW IT HAD A WAR ALL OF ITS OWN!

WE'VE GOT THE WHITE STUFF!

COMING, RED-DY OR NOT!

AT ONE TIME IT LOOKED LIKE THE WHITES WERE WINNING — SO THE BOLSHEVIKS HAD THE TSAR AND HIS FAMILY SHOT...

I'VE NEVER SEEN A SHOOTING TSAR!

LENIN TOLD THE BOLSHEVIKS TO TAKE CONTROL OF FARMS AND FACTORIES IN THE COUNTRY, AND GRAB WHATEVER FOOD THEY NEEDED FROM THE PEASANTS. THIS UPSET LOTS OF PEOPLE...

HAND OVER YOUR FOOD AND NOBODY GETS HURT!

DIDN'T YOU PROMISE US LAND, BREAD AND PEACE?

WHAT WE MEANT TO SAY WAS 'HAND OVER YOUR BREAD, PLEASE'

THE BOLSHEVIKS ALSO SET UP A SECRET POLICE CALLED THE CHEKA. THEY ARRESTED ANYBODY WHO ARGUED WITH THEM OR SUPPORTED THE WHITES...

I ONLY SAID I WAS DREAMING OF A WHITE CHRISTMAS...

...AND SENT THEM TO PRISON CAMPS IN SIBERIA.

BOLSHEVIK
THE ~~TSARS~~ PRISON CAMP

IN THE END THE BOLSHEVIKS BEAT THE WHITES. THEY RENAMED THEMSELVES 'THE COMMUNIST PARTY' AND TURNED THE TSAR'S RUSSIAN EMPIRE INTO THE UNION OF SOVIET SOCIALIST REPUBLICS (USSR).

THE USSR IS BORN

THIS PARTY DOESN'T LOOK MUCH FUN...

I AM THE NEW LEADER OF THE PARTY

BUT IN 1922 LENIN SUFFERED A STROKE (A BLOOD CLOT ON THE BRAIN) WHICH MADE HIM VERY SICK. STALIN SAW HIS CHANCE TO TAKE CONTROL...

WHAT A STROKE OF LUCK

URK!

BY THE TIME LENIN FINALLY DIED IN 1924, STALIN HAD PERSUADED EVERYONE THAT HE SHOULD BE THE NEXT BOSS OF THE SOVIET UNION.

I'M IN—STALIN MYSELF AS LEADER!

GULP!

THE RUSSIANS DIDN'T KNOW IT, BUT THEIR TERRIFYING TIMES HAD JUST BEGUN!

Bolshy Bother

It's 1920 and the Bolsheviks are in charge. Things are topsy-turvy – the workers are the bosses and the posh get pushed around! But thanks to the Civil War, everyone is hungry...

The Bolsheviks set up soup kitchens where people could get a meal. Roll up for weak cabbage soup and a lump of black bread – and hope the food doesn't run out while you're waiting in the queue!

If people didn't have fuel for their fires, a wealthy person's home would be chopped up for firewood.

OUCH! WE PRIESTS ARE EASY PREY!

YUCK! THIS WASN'T WORTH THE WAIT...

Bolsheviks believed that priests were 'parasites' who lived comfy lives while the people suffered. So priests were forced to do a proper day's work.

44

The Tsar's old guards had to clean up the streets at gunpoint – while their ex-servants stood around and laughed at them!

Living space in the cities was 'shared out equally' among all the people. What that usually meant was that posh folks got kicked out of their mansions – and worker's families moved in.

Bolshevik propaganda gangs went around putting up posters and announcing that the workers should terrorize the wealthy. 'Terrora' even became a popular name for girls!

DON'T FORGET TO SWEEP THE CORNERS! HA HA!

OOH, LOOK, TERRORA, THIS PLACE HAS A LOO!

WHO ATE ALL THE SAUSAGES?

HO HO! I AM A FACTORY OWNER WHO GETS RICH OFF THE BLOOD OF THE WORKERS!

WORKERS! PUNISH THE FAT CATS WHO OPPRESSED YOU!

YOU CAN HAVE IT FOR 5,000 ROUBLES – OR HALF A SLICE OF BREAD...

Nobles couldn't go to soup kitchens. Countesses and duchesses had to sell their most valuable possessions – just so they could buy some bread to eat.

FOR SALE

Plays were put on in the streets about heroic workers taking revenge on 'evil' factory-owners and priests. Some of the spectators even tried to get in on the action!

45

Pitiful for Peasants

The Bolsheviks didn't care much for country folk.
They made them work on enormous farms that were run like factories.
Welcome to a cruel 'collective farm'...

The Bolsheviks had changed the cities of Russia, and they were determined to change the countryside too. They did this by taking over hundreds of small farms and turning them into a few MASSIVE ones instead, called 'collective farms'. Stalin was particularly potty about them. Everything produced by these massive farms belonged to the government. The peasants were paid with just a small amount of food.

Russian to eat

Of course, collective farms were a dire disaster. The peasants' payment was so small they often starved. Across the whole of Russia, millions of people died. The Communists didn't care – they thought the people were being lazy. Besides, they didn't like peasants anyway!

DIDN'T WE HAVE A HORSE TO DO THIS?

WE ATE IT

REMEMBER – NO PAIN, NO GRAIN!

I'LL DIG YOUR GRAVE IN A MINUTE IF YOU DON'T SHUT UP

DIG FOR THE MOTHERLAND, COMRADES

IT'S A CASE OF STEAL OR STARVE!

1. The Bolsheviks made the farmers use tractors, but they didn't give them spare parts – so when the tractors broke down they were really in a rut.
2. If peasants were caught stealing grain, they would be sentenced to ten years in a labour camp or executed. But if you didn't steal any, you'd starve – the Bolsheviks took the rest!
3. Bolshevik bullies kept watch to make sure everyone did as they were told.
4. The Bolsheviks took all the grain, and sometimes forgot to leave any to be planted for next year's harvest!
5. Several farmers' families had to live together in one big room. Dozens of ill, hungry, sweaty peasants under one roof.
6. Big collective farms were given grand arches. But shiny signs and big red flags couldn't stop the weary workers from flagging.

The peasants knew that they were being used like slaves, but they didn't have any choice. Some smart peasants ate all their animals before the Communists could get to them.

Corn crimes

Those who survived did so by hiding food. But any peasant caught with their own property – even just a handful of grain – was called a 'kulak' (Russian for 'meanie') and executed. School bullies may call you nasty names, but at least they don't kill you.

CRUEL FOR KIDS

It wasn't just grown ups who were made to work for the Revolution. The kids were called up too. And they had to do some pretty mean things. Here are four of the worst...

Snitching titches

The authorities used kids to spy on their parents and report them for any wrong-doing. A kid could sentence his own parents to 25 years hard labour.

Party-loving kids

The Communist Party got keen kids to ride around all over the country in Bolshevik trains handing out leaflets and explaining why Communism (the Bolshevik way of life) was the best thing for the country.

Pull the other one

Kids were used to pull carts and carriages, because the horses that usually pulled them had already been eaten by the starving people.

Young guns

Orphans made keen recruits for the Red Army. At least in the army these kids might get a meal – before they got killed in the fighting, that is. How kind.

Red Riddles

1) Nasty Russian revolutionary Joseph Stalin had a wife but she died in 1932. What happened to her?

a) She choked to death on an American hamburger.

b) Stalin had her executed like so many others.

c) She killed herself because she was sick of Stalin.

JUST AS I THOUGHT. CAPITALIST FOOD IS BAD FOR YOU

2) The Bolsheviks had to fight a civil war to stay on top. Their troops were called the Red Army. What were their enemies called?

a) Black Russians

b) White Russians

c) Pink-with-blue-spots Russians

3) As a young man, Stalin had trained to be a...

a) Priest b) Assassin c) Maths teacher

4) Stalin came up with 'five-year plans' for making the country more efficient. How long were they supposed to take to carry out?

a) Four years b) Five years c) Six years

FIND THE FATE

The Russian Revolution was dangerous. If you were at the top, you might get the chop, no matter whose side you were on. Can you match these folks to their fates?

1) Leon Trotsky (rowdy revolutionary) — a) Beaten up

2) Nicholas II (terrible tsar) — b) Shot

3) Rasputin (mad monk) — c) Poisoned

4) Stalin (rowdy revolutionary) — d) Ice pick in the head

5) Grigory Zinoviev (rowdy revolutionary) — e) Drowned

6) Lev Kamenev (rowdy revolutionary) — f) Survived

Answers on pages 61.

48

Films, Flappers and Flights

Never mind all that beastliness in the East – what were folk doing for fun in the West?
Musical movies, marathon dances, deadly displays and dodgy dances, that's what!

While poor people in the USSR got used to severe life under Stalin, well-off folks in the USA were having a much better time. In 1920s America, there was a host of new fun things to do! These entertainments had their unfair and foul side, too…

1. Movies with sound! *The Jazz Singer* was the first film to have sound. But the star was white and painted his face to look like a 'minstrel' – a cruel cartoon version of a black entertainer.

2. Jazz clubs! Black people could be in the band, but they couldn't be members of the audience.

3. Dance contests! In the poor 1930s, dance competitions to win cash prizes became all the rage. People danced for up to six months! They should have called it 'The X-hausted Factor'.

4. Air shows! Daredevil flyers – 'Barnstormers' – performed stunts so risky… that they crashed.

49

Rockin' Riot

In Britain in the 1950s, a different kind of musical movie caused a right commotion. When 'Rock Around the Clock' hit the screens, teenagers screamed and got dancing, damaging and duffing! WARNING: oldies in your family might have been here!

'SHE LOVES YOU'

LET'S 'AVE A SLASH 'N A BASH!

THIS DIVE IS JIVING!

BUT I'M THE WILD ONE!

ANARCHY IN THE AISLES

1. When they felt the beat, the kids beat the felt seats! Cinema cushions got cut up with cut-throat razors.
2. Most 'rioters' were really just dancing. Rockers jived and writhed like lunatics with itchy pants.
3. Adults were terrified by this teenage trouble. Teenagers had become the new thing that everyone was getting bothered about. They thought the kids had gone off their rockers!
4. One teen tribe called 'Greasers' copied the motorbike-rider look and the fights they saw in a film called *The Wild One*.
5. Rumour has it the Queen (then 29) saw the film. Was she a rockin' ruler?
6. Gangs of 'Teddy boys' – who dressed up in a style based on Edwardian clothing – used the party to have punch-ups. Too bad if you'd picked the wrong colour socks!
7. Not everybody joined in the party. Old-fashioned ballroom dancers couldn't keep their feet in time to the crazy beat.
8. Bill Haley and the Comets were the film's shooting stars – even though singer Bill was old (30) and podgy.
9. Actors spoke over the title song – sending the kids rocking mad.

NO, 'ONE' IS THE WILD ONE!

I'M ROCKIN' ROUND THE CLOCK!

BAH! I'M QUITTING THIS JIVE DIVE

IT'S STRICTLY BORE –ROOM

I'M GONNA SOCK IT TO YOU

NOBODY'S LISTENING TO US

NO ICE CREAM ON THE SCREEN!

51

Silly Telly

Never mind the cinema... what's on the telly? In the 1950s the answer was...
not a lot! Here's an early TV guide...

The first TVs appeared in 1937, but they cost so much that few people could really afford them. Instead, everyone went to the cinema to see films or listened to the radio at home. The first proper broadcasting began before World War II but closed down for the six years of the war. When it started again in June 1946, the announcer began by saying "As I was saying before we were so rudely interrupted…"

TIME FOR BED

SQUARE EYES

Early TVs were monstrous. They had tiny screens and the wooden or plastic cases were usually hidden in a cabinet (people thought they were a bit common). The black and white picture didn't appear straight away – you had to wait for the set to 'warm up' first...

IS IT WARM YET?

I THINK IT NEEDS MORE COAL, SON

THAT'S IT DAD. HOLD IT THERE!

Some dads even made their own TVs by hashing together bits of old radars and electrical apparatus. Reception was usually lousy, and one family even had to go outside to get a picture.

Royal goggle box

By 1950, only 350,000 people could receive TV programmes, but things really got going in 1953 – because this was the year that Elizabeth II was crowned in Westminster Abbey. Everyone wanted to see Liz become Queen, but they couldn't all fit in the Abbey… so they bought TVs and watched it on that instead. Over 20 million people saw the coronation at home, at friends' or relatives' houses, or in cinemas and pubs.

Watch with Auntie

Pretty soon H-shaped aerials were appearing on rooves all over Britain. There was only one channel to watch – the BBC (The British Broadcasting Corporation), or Auntie as it was known. Why Auntie? Because the Beeb felt it had a duty to educate people – a bit like an 'Auntie knows best' attitude. (Flippin' cheek!)

Transmitters were switched on at 3pm on weekdays and 5pm on Sundays, and off for one hour at 6pm. The idea was to make it easier for mums to get toddlers off to bed… by tricking kids into thinking the TV had finished! (Typically selfish sneaky grown-ups'-type trick, that.) So just what could you watch?

Children's hour

Some programmes were especially for children. they were quite… simple. Andy Pandy (1950) ran for 20 years – with the same 26 episodes being shown over and over again. Boring!

The Beeb were big on puppets – after all, they were much cheaper to use than real people and you could get them to behave and talk exactly how you wanted. And how was that? Well, take Bill and Ben the Flowerpot Men (1952), for example.

It starred two characters made from flowerpots, and a 'sunflower' called Weed. They spoke a special language called 'Fer-lub-a-lub'. And some parents weren't very happy about it. They thought it was childish and that it would lead their children into bad habits with their own talking.

The other side

The Beeb had it all their own way until 1955 when ITV (Independent Television) started up. With it came advertisements for all kinds of new products, including one for a chocolate bar that was so light you could eat it between meals without spoiling your appetite.

(Do you really believe that?)
So what did TWO TV channels mean – more choice? No, more arguments, of course!

Live and kicking

One great thing about shifty 1950s TV was it was mostly live – which meant you saw when things went wrong. In a 1957 programme The Sky At Night, presenter Patrick Moore opened his mouth to speak and a fly flew in. He had to choose between spitting out the fly live on TV or swallowing it. He swallowed. But when he told his family about this later, he got no sympathy. They said that it was much worse for the poor fly!

The BBC's Blue Peter started in 1958. It's had more than its fair share of live disasters. One guest in the Eighties was a tortoise about to celebrate its 100th birthday. One of the presenters, Mark Curry, trod on it!

By the end of the 1950s, about 90% of the people in the UK could watch TV.

53

Musical Bumps

Beastly Boogies

Back in the twirling 1920s, there were loads of new dance styles — and some of them had nutty animal names. Here are seven of them — but which were real animal actions, and which are furred or feathered fakes?

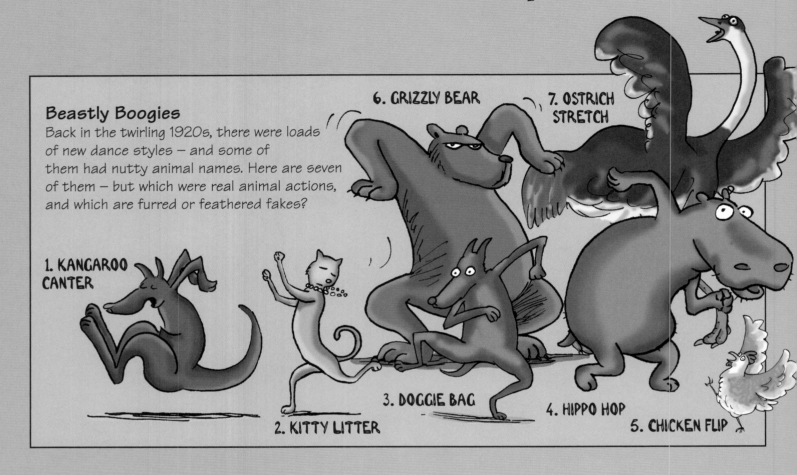

6. GRIZZLY BEAR

7. OSTRICH STRETCH

1. KANGAROO CANTER

2. KITTY LITTER

3. DOGGIE BAG

4. HIPPO HOP

5. CHICKEN FLIP

Skiffle Scuffle

In the 1950s, Britain's answer to American rock 'n' roll was … 'skiffle'. It was a kind of fast jazzy folk music — played on household objects! But can you guess which items being played below WEREN'T real skiffle instruments?

6. SINK PLUNGER

4. BIRDCAGE

2. COMB AND PAPER

5. JUG

7. WASHBOARD

3. SAW

1. TEA CHEST

54

Answers on page 6

Frosty Face-Off

Crazy music, movies and kids' programmes on TV all sound like peacetime fun, but then, weirdly enough, Britain got involved in one of the oddest wars ever – the 'Cold War'. Here's how things got so chillingly chilly. When the East and West faced each other out to see who was the best and biggest bully, the whole world was in a constant state of worry. It's a story of an 'iron curtain' and nuclear nasties...

AT THE END OF THE SECOND WORLD WAR, THE USA AND THE USSR* WERE THE MOST POWERFUL NATIONS IN THE WORLD...

HOORAY! THE WAR IS OVER!

YES, COMRADE! WE WON'T BE RUSSIAN TO FIGHT AGAIN!

*SEE PAGE 43!

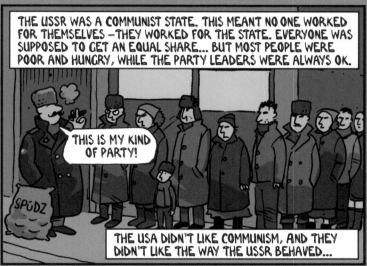

THE USSR WAS A COMMUNIST STATE. THIS MEANT NO ONE WORKED FOR THEMSELVES – THEY WORKED FOR THE STATE. EVERYONE WAS SUPPOSED TO GET AN EQUAL SHARE... BUT MOST PEOPLE WERE POOR AND HUNGRY, WHILE THE PARTY LEADERS WERE ALWAYS OK.

THIS IS MY KIND OF PARTY!

SPUDZ

THE USA DIDN'T LIKE COMMUNISM, AND THEY DIDN'T LIKE THE WAY THE USSR BEHAVED...

AFTER THE WAR, THE USSR GOT CONTROL OF THE COUNTRIES IN EASTERN EUROPE, AND SET UP COMMUNIST GOVERNMENTS IN THEM. THEY HAD HALF OF GERMANY TOO. (ITS CAPITAL, BERLIN, WAS DIVIDED UP AS WELL.)

GRR....

I GOT DIBS ON EASTERN EUROPE

EUROPE WAS DIVIDED IN TWO – THE 'FREE' WEST AND THE COMMUNIST EAST. THE BRITISH EX-PRIME MINISTER WINSTON CHURCHILL SAID IT WAS AS IF AN IRON CURTAIN HAD BEEN DRAWN ACROSS EUROPE.

IT'S CURTAINS FOR EASTERN EUROPE

PULL YOURSELF TOGETHER, COMRADE!

GERMANY

SO MANY PEOPLE ESCAPED FROM EAST BERLIN INTO WEST BERLIN THAT THE EAST GERMANS BUILT A WALL ACROSS THE CITY. BUT THAT DIDN'T STOP PEOPLE HAVING A GO. ONE MAN EVEN TRIED TO CLIMB OVER THE WALL ON A CLOTHES LINE!

YOU'RE ALL WASHED UP!

IT'S THE END OF THE LINE!

OOPS! I'VE BEEN HUNG OUT TO DRY...

MEANWHILE, THE USA'S FEAR OF COMMUNISM WAS GETTING OUT OF HAND. THEY HELD TRIALS OF ANYONE THEY THOUGHT MIGHT BE A 'COMMIE'.

ARE YOU A LYING COMMIE TRAITOR?

NO!

AHA! THAT'S JUST WHAT A LYING COMMIE WOULD SAY!

THE USA WAS SURE THAT IF THEY WENT TO WAR WITH THE USSR THEY WOULD WIN, BECAUSE THEY HAD NUCLEAR WEAPONS. JUST ONE OF THESE COULD DESTROY A WHOLE CITY.

THESE NUKES ARE A BLAST!

THE USA ALSO FORMED A GANG OF COUNTRIES CALLED NATO* TO STAND UP TO THE SOVIET UNION. THE GANG INCLUDED FRANCE, WEST GERMANY, THE UNITED KINGDOM AND CANADA.

HA HA! IVAN NO-MATES!

*NORTH ATLANTIC TREATY ORGANISATION.

BUT THEN THE USSR FORMED ITS OWN GANG OF COUNTRIES – THE WARSAW PACT – AND BUILT ITS OWN NUCLEAR WEAPONS.

IVAN IDEA YOU WERE WRONG!

THIS WAS THE BEGINNING OF THE 'ARMS RACE'. THE USA AND THE SOVIETS TRIED TO BUILD MORE NUCLEAR BOMBS, MISSILES, PLANES AND SUBMARINES THAN EACH OTHER...

WE HAVE ENOUGH NUKES TO KILL YOU FOUR TIMES OVER!

YEAH? OURS COULD KILL YOU TEN TIMES OVER!

ISN'T ONCE ENOUGH?

BOTH SIDES WERE ALWAYS SPYING ON EACH OTHER. THE SPIES MIGHT PRETEND TO WORK FOR THE OTHER SIDE. SOME EVEN SPIED FOR BOTH SIDES AT THE SAME TIME. VERY CONFUSING!

I'M NOT REALLY SPYING FOR US – I'M A DOUBLE AGENT WHO'S WORKING FOR THEM...

GOSH, SO AM I – I THINK...

AROUND THE WORLD, THE USSR AND USA PERSUADED POORER COUNTRIES TO FIGHT THEIR WARS FOR THEM BY SUPPLYING THEM WITH WEAPONS AND MONEY.

I'LL GIVE YOU GUNS AND CASH IF YOU BECOME COMMUNIST

PSSST – I'LL GIVE YOU EVEN MORE IF YOU DON'T!

HMMM...

THE TWO SIDES HAD ANOTHER RACE — TO EXPLORE SPACE. THE USSR GOT AN EARLY LEAD. IT SENT THE FIRST SATELLITE, THEN THE FIRST DOG, THEN THE FIRST MAN INTO SPACE...

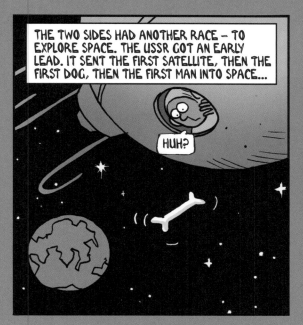

HUH?

THE COLD WAR GOT RATHER HOT IN 1963, WHEN THE USSR PUT SOME NUCLEAR MISSILES ON THE ISLAND OF CUBA, RIGHT NEXT TO THE USA.

UNITED STATES

GULF OF MEXICO

CUBA

WE CAN'T MISS FROM THIS ISLE!

THE US PRESIDENT, KENNEDY, THREATENED TO START A WAR IF THE MISSILES WEREN'T REMOVED. IN THE END, THE SOVIETS GAVE IN.

THE USA KEPT FIGHTING WARS AGAINST COMMUNISTS AROUND THE WORLD. IN 1965 THEY GOT INVOLVED IN A WAR AGAINST COMMUNISTS WHO WERE TRYING TO TAKE CONTROL OF VIETNAM. THE AMERICANS BURNED AND BOMBED THEM, BUT DIDN'T MANAGE TO BEAT THEM.

WHY DON'T THESE VIETNAMESE WANT TO BE OUR FRIENDS?

MAYBE WE SHOULD STOP BOMBING AND BURNING THEM...

IN 1969 THE AMERICANS FINALLY WON THE SPACE RACE WHEN THEY LANDED THE FIRST MEN ON THE MOON.

VIETNAM'S THAT BURNT BIT

THEN RONALD REAGAN BECAME PRESIDENT OF THE USA. HE SPENT BILLIONS OF DOLLARS BUILDING MORE WEAPONS. HE EVEN GAVE THE GO AHEAD FOR NUTTY NEW WEAPONS —GIANT SPACE LASERS TO SHOOT DOWN NUCLEAR MISSILES. (THEY NEVER GOT BUILT, THOUGH.)

RONNIE REAGAN? RONNIE RAY —GUN, MORE LIKE!

MEANWHILE THE COMMUNIST SYSTEM IN THE WARSAW PACT COUNTRIES WAS FALLING APART. IN 1989, IT COLLAPSED IN THE USSR. THE COLD WAR HAD JUST COST TOO MUCH.

COMRADE, CAN YOU SPARE A DIME?

THE USA HAD WON THE SILLY CHILLY WAR — BUT WITH MONEY, NOT MISSILES.

The Space Race

The Cold War wasn't just fought on Earth – it reached into space, too.
The Soviets and the Americans raced each other to put a man on the Moon...

MORE LIKE A CHUMP THAN A CHIMP

THOSE SOVIET DOGS ARE MAKING A MONKEY OUT OF ME

In the Cold War, both sides wanted to show that they were the best – particularly at science. They ended up in a crazy competition to put people into space. Before humans could be sent, scientists put animals in rockets to test whether they could survive. The Americans began with flies, but by 1949 they'd managed to send a monkey up. The Americans thought they were favourites to win the race. But their rockets could only go up into space and then fall apart. So they had a nasty shock when, in 1957, the Soviets launched a rocket that sent a satellite into orbit. *Race report: the Soviets are out of this world!*

Dog gone

The first animal in orbit was a Soviet dog called Laika (say ly-ka). Laika means 'barker' in Russian. She travelled in a spacecraft called Sputnik 2, so American journalists nicknamed her 'Muttnik'!

Unfortunately, at that time the Soviets could get spacecraft off the planet – but they couldn't get them back again. Laika died in space. *Race report: the Soviets have taken the lead!*

Top of the pups

The Soviets eventually built rockets that brought their dogs safely down to Earth. A female dog even had puppies once she'd got back. One of these was given as a present to US

ANY LAST REQUESTS LAIKA?

I'D LAIKA RETURN TICKET

President Kennedy. While the Soviets used dogs, the Americans got busy with other beasts. They sent a chimp called Ham into space and brought him back to Earth safely. Ham was rewarded with an apple and half an orange. Later that year another American chimp, called Enos, became the first monkey in orbit. *Race report: the chimps are no champs!*

Mice and Moon

Even more animals were sent to the stars. Americans sent up mice while the Soviets rocketed rats. The Soviets also sent a cargo of turtles, flies and worms to orbit the Moon. (Recently, the Americans sent a spider called Arabella into space to see if she could spin a web while she was weightless. She did, but no one told her there are no flies in space.) *Race report: it's like a zooming zoo up there!*

58

Out of this world

The Soviets got ahead again when they sent the first man into space – Yuri Gagarin. Yuri nearly didn't make it, though. The night before the flight, he and another cosmonaut (the Russian word for astronaut), Titov, were sent to bed. The scientist in charge decided to pick the man who slept best. Gagarin slept like a baby but Titov tossed and turned – so he wasn't picked!
Race report: the Russians are snoozing ahead!

Floating first

A Soviet cosmonaut beat the Americans to another first – going on a 'space walk'. This meant leaving the spacecraft while in orbit and drifting about on the end of a line.

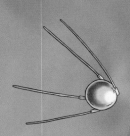

Launch break

But the Americans wanted to win the big race. They built a rocket the size of a 36-storey building to carry three astronauts to the Moon. The Soviets' big rockets kept exploding – or didn't take off at all.

Race report: the Americans have rocketed ahead!

Americans win!

Eventually, on 20 July 1969, two American astronauts made it to the Moon. The astronaut in charge, Neil Armstrong, had an especially prepared speech for the momentous moment as he stepped out onto the Moon's dusty, grey surface. He said…

Actually, what he really said was "This is one small step for man, one giant leap for mankind." He got it a bit wrong. He was supposed to say it was "One small step for <u>a</u> man." At least he discovered the Moon wasn't made of cheese. Mice everywhere were said to be very disappointed. *Race report: America's over the moon!*

Game over

The Americans landed on the Moon five more times – and then stopped visiting. No one has been back since. Instead, the Soviets started building space stations (science labs in space – not places for space trains to stop). The Americans weren't bothered – they knew they'd won the race.

DID YOU KNOW?

The first American manned space flight was only supposed to last for fifteen minutes - so short that they didn't think of fitting a toilet. But the launch was delayed for hours. The poor astronaut, Alan Shepard Jr, just had to wee in his spacesuit while he waited. So the first American in space went there in a wet suit. (The next astronaut wore a nappy!)

Answers

Highland Horrors (page 14)

The horrible truth is that they have ALL been played.

1) The Earl of Buchan (1380-1424) played the Hunt the Human, though he probably didn't call it that.
2) Tossing the Caber is still played at the Highland Games every year.
3) This was one of the events at the Invergarry Games of 1820 – along with "dancing, piping, lifting a heavy stone, throwing the hammer and running from the island to Invergarry and back"!
4) If you haven't got a dead horse, you can play 'hurley haaky' – if you have a haaky – a cow.
5) King Robert III (1337-1406) and a huge crowd gathered on the North Inch of Perth to watch two teams of 30 butcher each other.

How to Spot a Witch... (page 18)

All three are REAL reasons given for a spot of witch worrying.

Familiar Problem (page 18)

King James said that cats, dogs and even apes could be familiars – but lions were thought to be noble beasts. Unlike James.

Dress to Empress (page 30)

Amazingly, only one of these items wasn't worn by 19th-century African adventurers... the Y-fronts. Why? Because they hadn't been invented yet. In case you're wondering, the dress and petticoats were worn by a lady explorer called Mary Kingsley. She may have been camping out with gorillas in the Congo, but she was always perfectly proper!

Riverside Survival (page 36-37)

Hold on to your horrible hats – here they all are.

60

Crime Fines (page 40)

1) TRUE. A one penny fine on a man's land, a one pound fine on the road!
2) FALSE.
3) TRUE.
4) FALSE.
5) TRUE.
6) FALSE.
7) TRUE. James Wilson got away with a fine of two shillings and six pence (12p) for dressing as a woman.
8) FALSE.
9) TRUE.
10) FALSE.
11) TRUE. You could be fined up to £5 for dumping a dead animal, rotten meat or poo in the street.
12) FALSE.
13) TRUE. Throwing orange peel cost one young man a 12p fine in 1873 — and it's still a crime today.

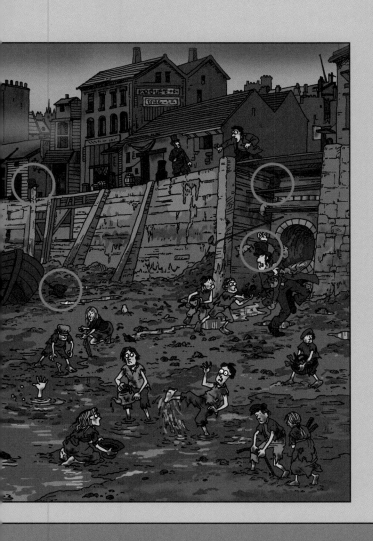

'Coster' That! (page 40)

The odd ones out are 'Daft Darren' and 'Smelly Sharon'. The rest are just odd.

Red Riddles (page 48)

1. c) 2. b) 3. c) 4. a) Thought that a five-year plan should take five years? Then you can't be working hard enough! Off to the gulag (a dreadful prison where anyone the Party didn't like was sent) with you!

Find the Fate (page 48)

1. d) 2. b) 3. a)… and b) and c) and e)! 4. f) 5. b) 6. b).

Beastly Boogies (page 54)

2. and 3. are bogus boogies, but the rest are all real names for dances from the 1920s.

Skiffle Scuffle (page 54)

Only 4. the Birdcage and 6. the sink plunger weren't ever used as real skiffle instruments. Can you imagine the racket the rest made? Yes, it was as bad as you think.

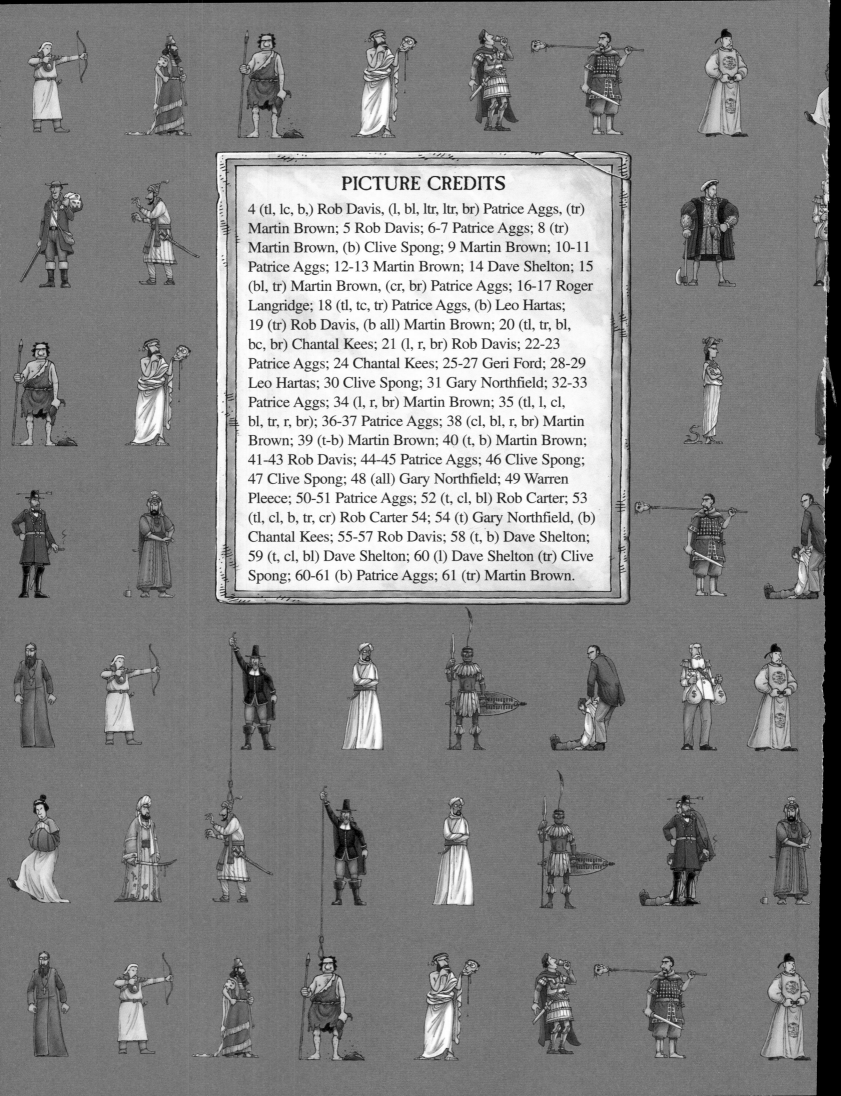

PICTURE CREDITS

4 (tl, lc, b,) Rob Davis, (l, bl, ltr, ltr, br) Patrice Aggs, (tr) Martin Brown; 5 Rob Davis; 6-7 Patrice Aggs; 8 (tr) Martin Brown, (b) Clive Spong; 9 Martin Brown; 10-11 Patrice Aggs; 12-13 Martin Brown; 14 Dave Shelton; 15 (bl, tr) Martin Brown, (cr, br) Patrice Aggs; 16-17 Roger Langridge; 18 (tl, tc, tr) Patrice Aggs, (b) Leo Hartas; 19 (tr) Rob Davis, (b all) Martin Brown; 20 (tl, tr, bl, bc, br) Chantal Kees; 21 (l, r, br) Rob Davis; 22-23 Patrice Aggs; 24 Chantal Kees; 25-27 Geri Ford; 28-29 Leo Hartas; 30 Clive Spong; 31 Gary Northfield; 32-33 Patrice Aggs; 34 (l, r, br) Martin Brown; 35 (tl, l, cl, bl, tr, r, br); 36-37 Patrice Aggs; 38 (cl, bl, r, br) Martin Brown; 39 (t-b) Martin Brown; 40 (t, b) Martin Brown; 41-43 Rob Davis; 44-45 Patrice Aggs; 46 Clive Spong; 47 Clive Spong; 48 (all) Gary Northfield; 49 Warren Pleece; 50-51 Patrice Aggs; 52 (t, cl, bl) Rob Carter; 53 (tl, cl, b, tr, cr) Rob Carter 54; 54 (t) Gary Northfield, (b) Chantal Kees; 55-57 Rob Davis; 58 (t, b) Dave Shelton; 59 (t, cl, bl) Dave Shelton; 60 (l) Dave Shelton (tr) Clive Spong; 60-61 (b) Patrice Aggs; 61 (tr) Martin Brown.